Editing and Revising Text

Jo Billingham runs courses in written communications. She
has worked with undergraduates and chief executives, and in
organizations as diverse as manufacturing and government
departments. She also writes and edits business-to-business
communications.

One Step Ahead …

The *One Step Ahead* series is for all those who want and need to communicate more effectively in a range of real-life situations. Each title provides up-to-date practical guidance, tips, and the language tools to enhance your writing and speaking.

Series Editor: John Seely

Titles in the series

Editing and Revising Texts	Jo Billingham
Essays and Dissertations	Chris Mounsey
Organizing and Participating in Meetings	Judith Leigh
Publicity, Newsletters, and Press Releases	Alison Baverstock
Punctuation	Robert Allen
Spelling	Robert Allen
Words	John Seely
Writing for the Internet	Jane Dorner
Writing Reports	John Seely

Acknowledgements

I would like to acknowledge the following people:
John Seely, the *One Step Ahead* series editor, for his instructive and detailed editor's comments on this book on editing. His perspective prompted many improvements.
Jessica Bisson and Siân Ellis for their valuable input to early drafts, which helped enormously in ensuring a reader focus.
The hundreds of trainees I have worked with, whose needs and interests prompted much of the content of this book.
And most of all my husband, Norman Billingham, for reading and re-reading, his academic knowledge, his patience, and support.

onestepahead

Editing and Revising Text

Jo Billingham

Cartoons by Beatrice Baumgartner-Cohen

OXFORD
UNIVERSITY PRESS

OXFORD UNIVERSITY PRESS

Great Clarendon Street, Oxford OX2 6DP

Oxford University Press is a department of the University of Oxford.
It furthers the University's objective of excellence in research, scholarship,
and education by publishing worldwide in
Oxford New York
Auckland Bangkok Buenos Aires Cape Town Chennai
Dar es Salaam Delhi Hong Kong Istanbul Karachi Kolkata
Kuala Lumpur Madrid Melbourne Mexico City Mumbai Nairobi
São Paulo Shanghai Singapore Taipei Tokyo Toronto
with an associated company in Berlin

Oxford is a registered trade mark of Oxford University Press
in the UK and in certain other countries

Published in the United States
by Oxford University Press Inc., New York

© Josephine Billingham 2002

British Library Cataloguing in Publication Data
Data available

Library of Congress Cataloging in Publication Data
Data available

ISBN 0-19-860413-0

10 9 8 7 6 5 4 3 2 1

Design and typesetting by David Seabourne
Printed in Spain by Bookprint S.L., Barcelona

Contents

1 | What is editing?

Introduction

Editing means different things to different people. Most office workers and students have to edit the text they have written. So do the many people who produce newsletters for clubs or community organizations. People edit reports, letters, and essays or electronic media, including emails and websites. They all want to make the text as good as they possibly can.

The editor of a newspaper or magazine is responsible for its appearance, and the view it takes on certain issues. These editors decide who they want to read the publication, and how to attract them. They will consider the style of writing to use, how complex the contents should be, and the extent to which they will use photographs, illustrations, and cartoons.

Between these extremes are all the employees who work on in-house magazines, marketing brochures, and newsletters.

Whatever type of document you are involved in editing, when dealing with the words (rather than appearance or policy) you will need to look at a number of areas.

Editor at Work

Why do we edit?

Writers edit what they have written, or edit each other's work, for a variety of reasons. We edit documents because:

- no matter how much we plan, the first version we write is unlikely to be perfect;

- the tone or mood of a document may not be as we intended it;

- there may not be enough space on the page for all we would like to say;

- we need to make a document suitable for a different group of readers;

- we want to make the content as clear as possible for our readers;

- longer documents often become dull and lose the readers' interest;

- although we use spelling and grammar checkers, there may still be mistakes;

- we need to apply our organization's 'rule books' on how language is used;

- it's essential to make sure facts, numbers, and names are all correct;

- some documents need extra help to entice the reader to keep on reading;

- we need to make sure that everything about the document is consistent, with itself and with other, similar documents;

- we want to be as concise as possible.

| # What do editors change?

The changes 'editors' make cover a variety of areas. For some people editing means tidying up a piece of text to make sure it's accurate and clear. Some 'editors' have to take long and complex documents and 'edit' them into simple brochures or manuals. While they call this 'editing', another person might call it 'rewriting'.

Corrections or
minor changes to detail

Major changes to content, structure, length, or style

Definitions don't always work

The difference between 'editing' and 'rewriting' is purely linguistic. Even the dictionary definition of 'editor' is too narrow to cover the type of work most editors have to do:

> **editor** (noun) **1** a person who is in charge of a newspaper, magazine, or multi-author book. **2** a person who commissions written texts for publication. **3** a person who prepares texts or recorded material for publication or broadcasting.
>
> *Compact Oxford Dictionary* (2000)

The barriers to communication

Whichever type of work editors do, they often think in terms of 'barriers' to communication. A 'barrier' is anything that gets in the way—forms an obstacle—between writers and the person or people they are writing for.

- Appearance
  People will not want to read a document which looks messy or uninteresting.

- Structure
  A structure which is hard to follow is an excuse to stop reading.

- Content
  If there's too much or too little information, or it's inappropriate, readers are irritated or confused.

- Lack of headings
  Long documents with no headings are hard for readers to find their way around.

- Inappropriate language
  Language which is old-fashioned, too technical or formal, or which uses jargon, discourages readers.

- Long, complicated sentences

- Long or complex words used solely to impress

- An inappropriate tone of voice

- Mistakes
  Errors in spelling, grammar, and punctuation will make the readers unlikely to trust your facts, figures, and analysis.

When does an edit become a rewrite?

Some people consider they are rewriting, rather than editing, if they have to rekey a large part of the text; others think they are rewriting when less than half the original text remains; yet others say that when you find you have to change the message or the tone of the piece, you are rewriting, not editing.

Editing

Rewriting

Whether you consider you are 'editing' or 'rewriting', the techniques you need to use and the areas you need to think about, will be the same.

Where does proof checking fit in?

See Part B on proof-checking

Proof checking is the final step in your editing. It is your final chance to spot mistakes, including the oddities put into the text by electronic transmission. It is a detailed, meticulous, and time-consuming task.

Proof checking is the final step in ∧editing.
∧ your

It's the final chance to spot mistaks,
∧ e

including the oddities put into the text by
𝟞𝟩

by electronic transmission.

𝟞𝟩 ∧ It is your

Allow time for the task

No matter which type of editing you are involved in, one of the most important things to remember is to allow time for the task.

Editing is not a luxury which you hope you will have time for before you hand in your essay or send off the letter.

Editing is not a luxury which you hope you will have time for before you hand in your essay or send off the letter. It is an essential part of putting your thoughts in writing. A document which has not been edited can give a bad impression of you, your department, or your organization—or all three. When planning to produce something in writing, always set aside some time to edit it before you send it off.

The more detailed the text, the longer your editing is likely to take. For example, a 1,000-word technical document containing a lot of figures and involving passages which need redrafting will take several hours. A 1,000-word essay which needs light editing may take under half an hour.

Always allow more time than you think you will need.

Step by step

Remember that, if you have an organized approach to editing:

■ you will be able to work more quickly;

■ you will be less likely to miss points.

This book gives you a stepped procedure. But always feel free to make your own choices when it comes to the task of editing, particularly when it comes to deciding when you edit on screen and when you edit on paper.

2

The different editing circumstances

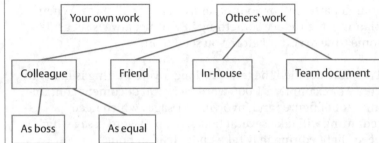

There are several different circumstances under which you could find yourself editing text. You may be editing:

- your own work, such as a letter or essay;

- a 'team' document, such as a report or proposal, or letters which colleagues draft on your behalf;

- pieces you request for in-house magazines or other publications;

- an unexpected piece sent into a club newsletter.

Editing your own work

You may not enjoy editing what you have written. Remembering how hard it was to write a piece originally, you will probably dislike crossing out the result of your efforts. It is also tricky because, when editing your own work, you will already be familiar with the text, which makes it more difficult to see how well or badly it reads.

As the writer of the text, you will know what you mean, so you may find it less easy to see where your readers would like more information or what they might misinterpret.

Also, most people have other tasks to do, whether they work in an office, are students, or edit a newsletter from home. They may be hard pressed to find time to edit the text.

Approaching your own work

■ If you have to edit a long document you have written, such as an essay or a newsletter, create a style sheet for yourself. Then you will not have to keep checking on areas such as how to abbreviate a word or which words you use capital initials for. For example, do you write 'per cent' or '%'? Do you write 'the club' or 'the Club'?

See Ch. 4, Style guides

■ Leave time between writing and editing. A general rule is: the longer and more complex the document, the longer the gap you should try to leave.

See Ch. 5, First steps

■ If you can't leave much time between writing and editing, do something completely different for a while (such as phoning or filing) to help you see the document afresh.

■ Before you start, remind yourself who the text is for, and what you set out to achieve with the piece.

See Ch. 3, Readers and aims

■ Be particularly aware of jargon which is so natural to you that you have forgotten that it might be meaningless to your readers.

■ When you read it through, 'hear' what you have written in your head. This slows down your reading, involves a different sense, and helps you to really take note of what is on the page.

■ Know what your own weaknesses are. For example, you may tend to use over-long, rambling sentences, miss out words, or be inconsistent.

See Part B, Editing a document as a team, for more ideas, and Ch. 14, How technology can help you

Do!

alter text because it does not conform to an agreed style, or the guidelines.

Don't!

alter text because it is not how you would have written it yourself.

See Ch. 4, Style guides, and Part B

When you are part of a team

Word-processing makes it easy for several people to work on a document and collate the information into one report or proposal. While that makes life easier in many respects, it can also create problems. Following a few guidelines—especially before you start—can make life easier.

Some of these guidelines are particularly important if people draft letters for you. When someone's work is constantly changed they lose confidence. They may even stop bothering to write a good draft because they know it will be changed.

Decide who 'owns' the document so that you know who has the final say, before writing begins. On larger documents, appoint an overall editor to be responsible.

Let people know if they should expect changes to what they have written, so that they realize that when something is 'changed' it isn't necessarily wrong. And let them know if you will show them any proposed changes.

If people write letters on your behalf and you send the drafts back to them for changing, explain which changes are a matter of style and which are to correct mistakes. They will be happier, will learn more and your job will become easier.

Make sure they are all thoroughly briefed about who the document is for, what it is setting out to achieve, and the preferred sentence length, use of capital letters, and layout. You can do this with a tailor-made style guide.

Editing documents you have requested

Many of the documents editors have to work on have been requested, such as articles for a house journal. As with team documents, many of the issues can be dealt with before writing begins. Make sure the writer knows who the readers are, and give them some guidance on style. You may be able to tell them what the piece should achieve, though that may be the writer's decision.

Before making a start, think about who the piece is aimed at and get yourself into their way of thinking.

Your first reading is the only time you will read the document the way your intended reader will read it. On other readings you will be familiar with the text. It is during this first reading that you are most likely to notice complex sentences, a confusing structure, or excessive detail.

If you make changes and correct mistakes during this first reading, you risk losing the impact of the text. Instead, read the piece through in the way the reader will—glance at headings, flick through the pages, or read it through quickly.

Dealing with unexpected editing work

If you edit an in-house magazine or club newsletter, colleagues and members may send you articles which will need editing. As you are likely to rely on them to keep you supplied with information, it's particularly important to apply a few extra rules:

■ acknowledge what they have sent to you;

■ let them know why you decide to use it or not use it;

■ explain why you have made changes.

 Do!

read as the intended audience.

 Don't!

pause to correct minor mistakes.

3 Readers and aims

Do!

make sure you think about the basics before you start to edit.

Keys to good editing

There are two principles which should guide your editing, whatever type of text you work with.

| Who is the document intended for? | What does it aim to achieve? |

Your answers to these questions will influence the changes you make to:

■ the content;

■ the way you present the information;

■ the type of language you use.

If you are working on your own text, you should have been clear about who your readers will be and what your aims are before you started to write. Editing is another chance to make sure that you have presented the information appropriately. If you work on text written by other people, they should let you know who the document is for, to help you edit it in an appropriate way. They may want to leave you to work out what the document seems to aim to achieve. This is one way of checking whether the document really does do its job.

Readers and aims are such an important guide to editing and revising that both questions need thinking about in detail.

Who is the document for?

You need to know as much as possible about the person, or people, who will read the text you are editing. The more you know about them, the more appropriate you can make it for them.

The points you will need to know about include:

■ your readers' knowledge of the subject;

See Part B for a checklist of points you may want to know about your reader

■ their attitude to the subject, the argument, or your organization;

■ how they want to work with the document.

What if you don't know a great deal about your readers?

If you do not have a lot of information about your readers, but many of the questions in Section B of this book seem relevant, find out the answers, through research or, if appropriate, by asking the readers themselves.

When it's not possible to find out about your readers, you have to compromise.

If it's not possible to find out about your readers, you have to compromise. Answer as many of the questions as you can. You may be able to guess some of the missing answers. A guess is more likely to help you edit than not thinking about the point

What if the document is for a range of people?

Some documents, such as an election manifesto, go to a range of people and they all need to be able to understand it. When this is the case, think about 'groups'. You may find you have *groups* of readers whom you can keep in mind while editing. This should help you make sure that everyone understands the text, and can take from it the information they need.

See Part B on editing the technical for the non-technical

Why is it so important to know about the reader?

See Ch. 6, Editing the content

Once you fully understand what your reader is like, as the editor or writer-editor you can:

■ add to or delete from the text, according to their needs;

■ decide the best way of communicating, for example with diagrams, bullet points, or short sections;

■ choose an appropriate level of language, such as deciding what might be considered 'jargon'.

Small changes can bring big improvements

Watch out!
Edit text to suit your audience, not yourself.

The changes you make to a piece of text can be quite subtle.

The following passage, which is about donations to charity, is fine for people who deal with tax matters all the time and are used to this way of communicating.

> Provided an employee pays, or will pay, basic rate tax on his or her own income in the tax year in which the date of payment falls, and that tax equals or is greater than the basic rate tax on the donation, then he or she will need to pay no more tax in respect of this gift.

For people who are less used to dealing with tax matters, the following version would be more appropriate.

> You do **n o t** have to pay more tax in respect of this gift:
>
> ● if you have paid, or will pay, basic rate tax on your own income in the tax year in which the date of payment falls, **and**
>
> ● if that tax is equal to, or more than, the basic rate tax on the donation.

What does the document aim to achieve?

Every piece of text sets out to achieve something. If you look around you, you will probably see words on all sorts of things: buses, food wrappings, newspapers, pens, computers. All those words are being used to achieve something: to inform, advertise, label, warn . . . there is no end to the list. Even single words are being used to achieve something.

Every document you edit will have a purpose.

- 'Schiphol' informs you where the plane is going.

- 'Pepsi'® advertises the drink, and labels the can.

- 'DANGER' warns you not to approach an area.

Every document you edit will have a purpose, and it is part of the editor's job to make sure the document achieves it.

Know the aim

Most documents have a combination of aims. Some of these will be broad aims—aims which are general and can be applied to most pieces of text. The text you are editing may have a single or a principal *broad* aim, or it may combine many of the broad aims. Broad aims include the wish to:

- inform

- persuade

- interact

- entertain

- find out

- regulate/control

- record

People who edit company or club newsletters often overlook the need for every piece to have an aim.

Do!

know what you want your document to achieve.

You will have specific aims

With some documents, it's obvious what the specific aim is: a sales letter aims to sell something; a proposal recommends a certain line of action; an invoice invites someone to pay.

With some text, the aim is less obvious, but there will still be one. A business letter may aim to make sure the reader understands or accepts decisions. A memo about procedures may aim to persuade people to change the way they work.

People who edit company or club newsletters often overlook the fact that every piece of text should have an aim. For example, an article about a new product or service may aim to convince readers that the company is enterprising, and to thank those who worked on the launch. In a club newsletter, an account of a social event could aim to remind people what a good time they had and to encourage those who weren't there to go to the next function.

Your specific aims could include the wish to:

- sell a product or idea

- thank people

- alter behaviour

- change beliefs or perceptions

- obtain a meeting with someone

- build a relationship

- obtain support

You need to be sure of the aim of the document you are editing or revising. If *you* don't know the aim, or can't identify it in someone else's work, it could be a matter of chance whether the reader extracts the intended meaning from the text.

Why is it so important to make the aim clear?

If you present information to people and leave them to draw their own conclusions they may miss the point. People who are busy often do not read very thoroughly, and may not arrive at the conclusion you hoped for.

Also, when you are clear about the aim of the text, you may decide that some information can be omitted. When you do that, the text becomes shorter, more likely to be read, and even more likely to achieve its aim.

If you make sure the text supports your aim, your readers will be more likely to react the way you want them to react.

Students take note

These points apply in a different way to academic writing.

Students are in the unusual position of writing for people who know more about the subject than they do. They are usually presenting facts or ideas which the reader already knows, unless they are writing doctoral or master's theses which describe new work.

The reader's high level of existing knowledge makes it even more important to present the facts and ideas in an interesting and logical way, and this should be a major consideration in your editing. With an essay, you should be clear about your aim. If you want to put across an opinion, you should make sure that it comes across clearly. You may choose to state your view at the start, and then support it in the rest of your writing. Alternatively, you may want to discuss a subject before drawing your conclusions at the end.

You will certainly hope your essay shows your knowledge, the breadth of your reading, or depth of your analysis. Whichever you are doing, and you may be doing all three, make sure you have those aims in mind while you edit and revise.

Dealing with diverse readers

It is difficult to edit a document effectively when the text is intended for readers who have different levels of knowledge or experience of the subject you are dealing with, or when the text is for a range of age groups or people with different reading abilities.

See Part B for Know your readers checklist

While some people edit so that the text is right for those with the lowest level of understanding, this can lead to those who are more familiar with the subject feeling that the document is not relevant to them, or they may consider that you are talking down to them.

Another frequent practice is to edit for the middle range of readers. The danger here is that people who know a lot about the subject still feel bored; those who are unfamiliar with the subject can still feel confused.

The best way to deal with this difficult situation is to realize that your role as editor is to help the less knowledgeable readers by giving them additional information or help, which some of your readers may not need. Once you recognize this is what you need to do, you can choose the best technique to use.

Your role as editor is to help the less knowledgeable readers by giving them additional information.

You may decide:

- to give your readers extra help at the start of the document;

- to feed extra information to them slowly, as they read through the document;

- to combine these two ways.

Ask some extra questions

If your document is going to a diverse range of people, you will find the task easier if you ask yourself some additional questions.

- Why will all these people receive the document?

- What connects these readers? Do they all live in the same road? Work for the same organization? Do they all want to change in a particular way?

- What concerns do they share?

The answers will help you to clarify what changes to make. There are then a number of techniques you can use to help all your readers understand the text.

Techniques to try at the start of the document

Add a special section

A special section for your less knowledgeable or less technical readers can help them to catch up with their more experienced colleagues. The section could be headed 'Background', 'History', or, in less formal documents, 'All you need to know about ... '. Whatever you decide to call this section, you should make it clear in the heading that some readers might not want to read this part of the text.

Supply a glossary

A glossary is an alphabetical list of words which are used in the text, with brief explanations. A glossary is often placed at the end of the document, but there is no reason why you cannot place one at the start if your readers will find that more helpful. If you do this, put an asterisk (*) in the text alongside any word explained in the glossary.

Techniques to help people as they read the text

Use footnotes

Footnotes are easily created on many word-processing packages and are useful for highly detailed information. They provide, in a convenient place, the facts that some readers need. However, they may make a document appear studious or heavy.

Use appendices in reports

Use the appendix of a report for supporting information, and always make it clear in the body of the text that you have provided more detailed information at the end.

You may put your glossary in the appendix, rather than at the start of the document. If you do this, make sure your reader is aware that this helpful information has been provided.

Use boxes

Do!

put facts in boxes. They are very helpful.

You can put supporting facts in a box, on the same page as the rest of the information. This allows readers to refer to helpful material easily, and boxes can make a page look more interesting. Suitable details for 'boxing' could be product descriptions, software uses, or essential background.

Use brackets

Editors can add brief explanations in brackets. However, too many brackets can make documents seem difficult and inaccessible. Consider putting definitions and descriptions in brackets. They are also the best method of explaining acronyms (abbreviations created by using initials only, such as ROM, RAM, and CAD). You need only do this if some of your readers will not understand the abbreviation.

Be visual

Graphics can make some subjects easier to follow. If your text involves a lot of figures, consider using a graph or pie chart. Everyone will find them easier to understand than lists of figures, and they make your text look more inviting.

Use charts

If you are editing a document that explains a process, such as how an office handles its paperwork, a flow chart can help to explain it. Other types of chart can show how parts of a process are linked or overlap.

Test the end product

With difficult or technical text, always test the end document on people who have a similar level of knowledge and understanding to your intended readers. They will be in a strong position to give you valuable feedback and advice.

Borrow good ideas

Whenever you read anything technical or complex which you feel communicates particularly well, notice how the writer and editor have put the information across. You may be able to adapt the ideas for your own editing tasks.

And into the future

Provide details about where and how people could obtain information. Possibilities include:

- a contact number, such as a helpline;

- other publications produced by a company or group;

- a bibliography of further reading on the subject;

- training courses which would help people.

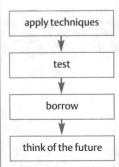

25

4 Style guides

See Part B, Style
guides and Style
guide checklist

 Do!

make sure you are
comfortable with
the brief before you
start to edit.

What a style guide is

A style guide is document which helps writers and editors by answering many of the questions they will meet when editing. They vary enormously in length, complexity, and formality, and could be anything from a published book to a few typed pages which you use as a checklist. The content may cover such areas as the linguistic and knowledge level the text should assume and the tone that the document should have. A useful aspect of a style guide is that, where there is a choice about the way something is expressed, it can provide the preferred option, such as:

- the use of capital initials (*manager* or *Manager*);

- the use of symbols (*per cent* or *%*), *italics* and **bold**;

- preferred spellings (*focussed* or *focused*).

In some roles, you may be given a written brief. Whether you are an editor or a writer-editor, be sure that the brief answers all the questions you need to know. If it doesn't, ask for more detail. The checklists in Part B will help you. Before you start to edit, you need to be confident about:

- the readers, including their linguistic and knowledge level;

- the aims of the piece, or of the overall publication;

- special issues, such as past problems.

Why you need a style guide

There are many advantages to having a style guide to refer to.

■ As decisions about points of detail are made just once, they can save editors a lot of time.

■ They help to ensure that documents are consistent, which contributes towards creating a professional image.

■ When several people are contributing to a document, they help the individuals to work together more efficiently.

■ Your role may involve editing different publications for a number of audiences, such as staff, customers, and share-holders. In such cases, a style guide helps you to focus on the different groups.

Ready-made style guides

Many large organizations have a style guide or approved house style. This is often produced by the marketing or public rela-tions specialists. It may be a manual covering every imaginable question related to putting words into print, from using trade marks to common grammatical errors. Other organizations have short style guides, sometimes just a few sheets of paper, which answer the day-to-day questions which arise when people are writing or editing

If your organization has a style guide or house style, follow it—unless you are confident that you are dealing with an exception. For example, the guide may say that product names must be written in full, but if working on an internal publication you may be able to abbreviate the names.

See Part B for Style guide checklist

There are many published style guides which are useful for refer-ence, including those produced by newspapers and periodicals.

Always remember your reader.

Creating your own style guide

Whatever type of text you edit, if you do not have a style guide you may want to invest time in producing your own. Whether you work on your own or with other people, a style guide will:

■ save time;

■ aid consistency and professionalism.

Include the essentials

It is worth beginning your style guide with a reminder about whom the text is intended for, and what their linguistic preferences are likely to be. This could include a note that, for the reader of the type of document you are working on, a certain type of vocabulary or sentence length is appropriate.

See Part B, Style guides and Style guide checklist

Develop the detail

To develop the detail of your style guide, start by noting down all the points which you find you query when you are editing. Then, decide how you are going to answer the questions, such as which spellings and symbols you prefer.

There's a list of areas which style guides frequently cover in Part B. You will want to add to this list other points which are specific to the type of editing you do.

You will probably find that your list of points keeps growing. This is excellent, as it means you are becoming a more efficient editor.

Obtain approval

If the style guide is to help you in academic writing, or if you are the editor of a newsletter who works alone, your style guide will be for your use, and your use only. In this case you can make your own decisions, so long as you bear in mind your readers' preferences.

If you work for an organization, you may want to start creating a style guide which you will eventually get approved for use by everyone in your department or throughout your organization.

Let your word processor help you

An editor's style sheet is different from those offered by many word-processing packages. These deal with the appearance of a document by applying your chosen sizes and fonts for headings and other aspects of layout.

See Ch. 14, How technology can help you

Editors who work on screen may find they can customize the auto-correct part of their word-processing packages to help apply some of the 'rules' which they prefer to follow in editing.

But beware!

Be cautious about relying on your word processor to deal with points which you should really be thinking about yourself. Word processors are certainly quick and convenient, and that sometimes creates the impression that they are more clever than they are. When it comes to editing text, there is no substitute for the human brain, and thought.

When it comes to editing text, there is no substitute for the human brain, and thought

5 | First steps

See flow chart on Editing: the process, p. 33

The number of edits

The more you read a piece of text, the less likely you are to be able to judge how well it communicates. So it makes sense to keep the number of edits you do to a minimum, especially if you have a deadline.

There are differences between editing your own and another person's text.

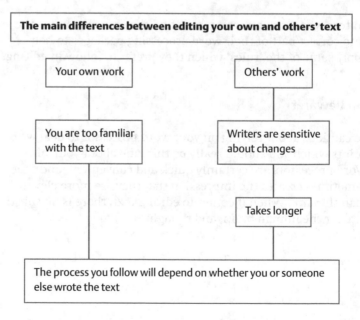

The main differences between editing your own and others' text

Your own work — You are too familiar with the text

Others' work — Writers are sensitive about changes — Takes longer

The process you follow will depend on whether you or someone else wrote the text

You decide the process

As editing is an individual activity, editors and writer-editors usually want to decide for themselves how many times to edit a document. But try to limit the number of edits you do. Your decision will usually be related to:

■ the length of the document;

■ the complexity of the content;

■ the amount of change it needs.

Editors like to choose the order in which they do the edits. As brevity, tone, and clarity are linked, you may want to edit them at the same time.

See Ch. 11, Brevity, and Ch. 12, Clarity

Spelling and punctuation should be edited separately. If you check them while you are editing other areas, you risk missing something. Deal with them last, so that you do not spend time correcting text which you decide later to leave out.

Watch out!
If you try to check content, flow, spelling, and punctuation all at the same time, there's a good chance you'll miss something.

Be prepared

When you have a piece of text to edit, try to work on it at the time of day that is best for you, and find a place where you won't be interrupted.

■ make 'clean' copies of the text, on paper or on disk, so that you can return to the original if you are in doubt about any of the changes you are considering;

See Ch. 5, and Part B for list of items in the editor's toolkit and more about style guides, including a checklist

■ assemble everything you need with you before you start, including reference books, writing materials, any earlier drafts, and the style guide, if you have one;

■ take another look at the brief or the essay title;

■ think about your reader.

The first look through

See Ch. 16, How technology can help you

Avoid making immediate changes when you first look through the text, because you lose the chance to take in its overall impact. Just glance at the text, especially if it's a long document, asking yourself:

■ Does it seem appealing?

■ Is it well divided up?

■ If so, do the parts or sections follow on logically?

Then read the text, and highlight or mark anything that jumps out at you, whether it's clumsy sentences, confusion, or errors. These will be areas to return to. If you are working on screen, your software package will probably allow you to highlight or underline the changes you make, or want to make.

Want to know more?

See Ch. 6

■ Content—does it cover all the relevant points?

See Ch. 9

■ Tone—is it appropriate for the purpose?

See Ch. 10

■ Accuracy—are the facts correct and supported?

See Ch. 11

■ Brevity—are there wasted words and phrases?

See Ch. 12

■ Clarity—is the language used plain and clear?

On screen or on paper?

 Do!

experiment with editing the same piece of text both on screen and on paper. Using both methods you are much more likely to spot what you need to change.

Most editors prefer to work on paper rather than on screen, as editing on screen is tiring. Also, people 'see' text differently when it's printed. Which way you work—on screen, paper, or a combination of both—is a personal preference. It would be wrong to change your natural inclination for the sake of it.

Editing: the process

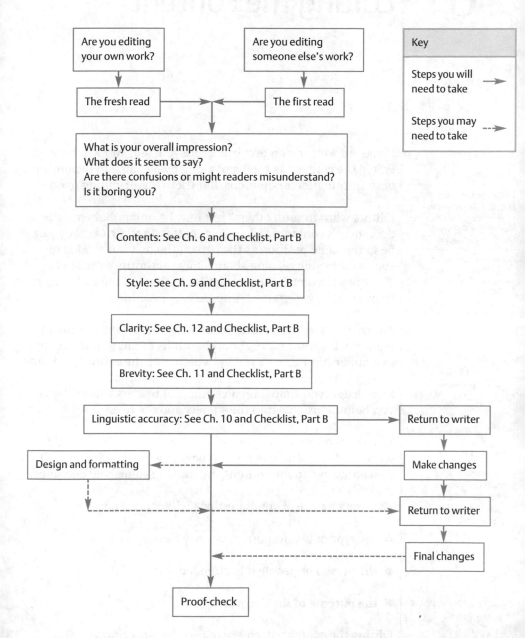

Are you editing your own work?

Are you editing someone else's work?

Key

Steps you will need to take →

Steps you may need to take --→

The fresh read

The first read

What is your overall impression?
What does it seem to say?
Are there confusions or might readers misunderstand?
Is it boring you?

Contents: See Ch. 6 and Checklist, Part B

Style: See Ch. 9 and Checklist, Part B

Clarity: See Ch. 12 and Checklist, Part B

Brevity: See Ch. 11 and Checklist, Part B

Linguistic accuracy: See Ch. 10 and Checklist, Part B

Return to writer

Make changes

Design and formatting

Return to writer

Final changes

Proof-check

6 | Editing the content

See Part B, The
'editing contract'

 Do!

involve specialist
readers if you are
uncertain about
your knowledge
of the subject.

*But screw your courage
to the sticking-place,
And we'll not fail.*

(Macbeth I.vii.60)

If you are working on text you wrote yourself, you will have edited the content as you went along by deciding to include or omit information or opinions. But there is still editing to do.

Editors who work on others' text may be unfamiliar with the document's contents and subject matter. In this case, they *may* be in the same position as the person the text is intended for, such as someone reading about a local authority's decisions. Their reactions may then be similar to those of the end reader: they could be entertained, impressed, or confused.

Alternatively, editors sometimes work on text which is for readers who know more about the subject than they do, such as a publication about a hobby, which puts the editor at a disadvantage. If you feel uneasy about your level of subject knowledge, you should involve external readers who will give you helpful insights into the subject and the text.

Whether you are an 'editor' or a 'writer-editor' who is familiar with the document, you need to begin by looking at it overall, concentrating on the content and making some bold decisions.

The exact nature of your questions will depend on:

■ the type of text (report, essay, newsletter);

■ the person or people it is intended for;

■ the purpose of the document.

Editing the content of a piece of text requires courage. The changes you make at this stage can be large and dramatic.

You could be forced to admit that pieces of text you laboured over should really be omitted. You may also find that quite large pieces of text need completely rewriting.

See Ch. 3, Readers and aims

There are good reasons for editing the overall content of the text first.

■ You need to look at the whole, before you examine the detail.

■ You don't want to work on text you may later delete.

■ Any additions, or deletions, tend to make other changes necessary. So, dealing with the 'big picture' first helps you cut down the number of times you go through the text.

First questions

As you start to edit the text, ask yourself some questions.

■ Does the document meet the brief or answer the question?

■ Does it differentiate between fact and opinion?

■ Is there is too much information?

See Part B: Contents checklist

■ Is there is too little information, causing confusion or mis-understanding?

■ Is it truthful and meticulous about differentiating between fact and opinion?

■ Is there a better way to communicate this?

This will help you to decide what to do about the content of each sentence, paragraph, and section. Your answers enable you to go on and answer the following questions about the content.

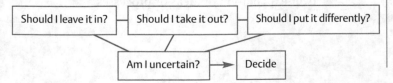

| Should I leave it in? | Should I take it out? | Should I put it differently? |

| Am I uncertain? → Decide |

Deciding whether the text fits the brief

Most people have had the experience of answering an exam question or carrying out a piece of work and realizing— often too late—that they haven't done what was asked of them.

Check back to the brief or the question before you begin to edit, and frequently during the editing process if the document is long. If you are working on someone else's text, make sure you find out whom it's for. Decide whether you should be told its aim, or should work out yourself what its aim appears to be.

You may find it worth writing down the question or the brief and putting it somewhere, such as on a notice board, where you can refer to it constantly. Keep asking yourself:

| Is this relevant? | → | Am I sure? |

When you have too much information

When a piece of text is too long, it usually looks it. Busy people find that daunting and it may prevent them reading the text. Over-long documents may bore people, and they often include elementary information which seems patronizing.

If you need to make your document shorter, look for:

■ repetition of facts or opinion;

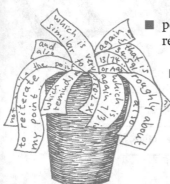

    ■ points where the text digresses into areas which are related, but not relevant;

      ■ high levels of detail that is unnecessary for the readers and purpose of this particular document;

    ■ over-explanation of ideas or processes.

Not sure?

When editing, it's not always easy to decide whether or not something should be included in the text. These are points which come under the heading of 'nice to know', rather than 'essential' or 'not important'.

If you find it hard to decide whether to include something, ask yourself:

■ Do these readers already know this?

■ What is the worst thing that could happen if I leave out this information?

■ Is this information easily available elsewhere?

If there's a need for more information

If documents contain too little information they may cause misunderstanding or confusion; mistakes or wrong decisions may be made if readers haven't grasped the full meaning of the text. Sometimes a good idea needs more 'proof' to support it.

Editors have to balance the need for more information against the disadvantage of making the document longer. But it is essential to include all the necessary information. You may want to add to a document by providing:

■ summaries of points, ideas, or arguments;

■ examples, quotations, or figures to support the point;

■ definitions of terminology with a glossary of terms;

■ additional headings or sub-headings.

 Do!

balance the readers' need for enough information with the fact that they would probably prefer a short document.

Bridging the gap

When you have to add to the text, who writes the extra material? If you are editing your own work, the writing is obviously up to you. Try to note what's needed and carry on editing rather than writing new text immediately,

When you are editing another's work, you may prefer them to write the new text. If so, explain why you consider there's a gap, and how it should be filled.

Is there a better way to communicate?

Text is just one way of putting across information, and it may not be the best way to help readers grasp the meaning accurately and quickly. Writers and editors have a mass of ways to communicate thoughts or ideas. Although the method of communication should be decided before writing begins, editing is an opportunity to consider the other methods, such as:

- ■ diagrams, graphs

- ■ lists of points

- ■ maps, plans, charts

- ■ photos, drawings, illustrations

- ■ calculations or tables of figures

- ■ 'boxed' information

- ■ highlighted text

- ■ drop-in quotations

On-screen editors

Editors working on screen may find their software can help with many of these alternative communication methods.

✔ **Do!**

think about other ways to put the point across—not just text.

See also Ch. 14, How technology can help you

Assessing the content

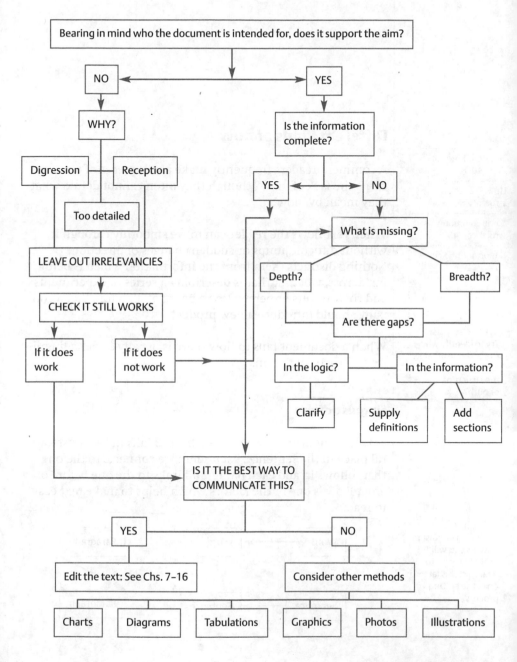

7 Achieving structural flow

Spot the cause
Try to identify why
the text doesn't flow.
Is it the language,
the structure,
or both?

Different kinds of flow

A comment readers frequently make about pieces of text concerns the lack of 'flow', though they often cannot define what they mean by 'flow'.

When text flows the reader can move smoothly through it, without difficult jumps or sudden changes of direction. Nothing distracts them from the information which is being put across, whether that is describing a series of experiments and their results or persuading a board of directors that a company should introduce a new product.

When a document fails to flow there is usually either a linguistic or structural reason.

Linguistic flow

See Ch. 8,
Achieving linguistic
flow, as you will
probably want to
deal with this later
on in the editing
process.

Text has linguistic flow when each word falls in the most natural place in the sentence; each sentence connects to the one that follows it, and each paragraph links to the one before or after. Flow is one of the factors which helps to make text easy to read.

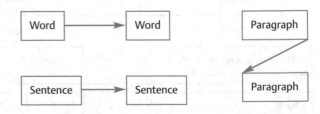

Structural flow

Structural flow is closely related to content, which is dealt with in the previous chapter.

See Ch. 6, Editing the content

Editing the *content* involves ensuring that all the points and opinions included are relevant, and communicated in the best manner.

Editing the *flow* means making sure that every part of the document is in the most effective place, so that each section or passage connects with the one before, and the one after it.

How to check if structure flows

When a document flows it is easy to follow the writer's logic, argument, or points. Often, the document will be well signposted, indicating where there's a change of direction. This may be done by using headings or section numbers; in essays, a point might be summarized before moving on.

When you are reading text on screen, such as part of an inter- or intranet site, you often have to connect to a different part of the site to find the information you want. Again, you will need to provide links and signposting, so that your readers do not lose the sense of flow as they move around the site.

Structural signposts can include:

- contents page
- introduction
- headings
- sub-headings
- section numbers
- cross-references
- summaries of points or arguments
- interim conclusions
- diagrams of document's structure

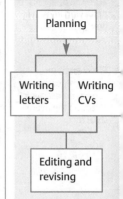

Working with your own text

If you are working with your own text, you should have ensured the structure flowed before you began writing.

If you want to be sure that the structure you have used really has achieved the sense of flow you are aiming for:

■ leave a gap between writing and editing;

■ apply the same techniques as you would to someone else's text.

Working with others' text

Spot the cause
Ask yourself whether the piece lacks flow because the writer hasn't connected different parts of the text.

See Ch. 8, Achieving linguistic flow

Remember
Even a minor change can have a dramatic affect on the overall structure.

As you read through text written by others, ask yourself how well it seems to flow.

- Do you feel confused by what you are reading?

- Are there jumps in the logic?

- Does the text change direction without warning, so that you do not immediately realize that the writer has moved on to another area or point?

- Does the writing make the author's meaning clear?

- If the 'destination' of the text isn't clear, does it matter? You may be happy to be intrigued about where the text is leading, as we are with novels, particularly detective fiction.

- Is there text which should be omitted?

If you feel confused by the flow of the argument, or if the text seems to jump from one point to another, it could be that the sections or blocks of information could be put into a more effective order.

Alternatively, it could be that the order is correct. The confusion could be because the writer has failed to underline the connection between different parts of the text. To put this right, you need to make changes to the *linguistic* flow, which is dealt with in the next chapter.

There are some basic structures which writers often follow. You may want to check to see if the writer has followed one of these, or a similar structure which you can then emphasize. Or you may feel you need to reorder the text to comply with one of these structures.

Some commonly used structures

Linear

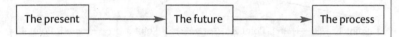

This takes the reader in the most direct route through the text. It might explain a current position (the present), the ways in which the writer would like to see the situation change (the future), and the steps which would be needed to make the changes (the process).

Comparative

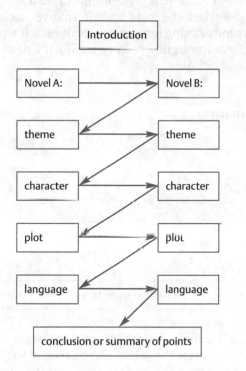

This would typically be used when comparing alternatives, such as two novels. The structure may deal with novel A, then novel B. Or it could compare different aspects of the books alternately, moving between novels A and B, as shown in the chart.

Developmental

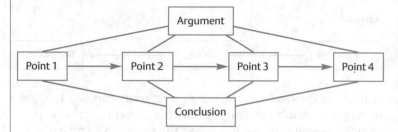

In this structure, the writer introduces the subject or argument of the text, and then supports it with a number of points, before reinforcing the argument at the end in the conclusion. For example, the document could start by stating the need for more staff, and then present information about long hours being worked, the costs, and alternatives such as allowing overtime or using temporary employees. It would then reinforce the argument by re-stating the need for more staff, in the conclusion.

Thematic

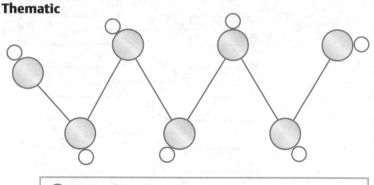

○ shows related subjects ——— shows the linking theme

In this structure, there is a theme—shown by the green line—which connects the points. Other, related subjects—the small spheres—could also be dealt with, but they are not part of the main thrust of the text. For example, the main theme could be how a sports team has improved its performance. Related subjects could be new training schedules or supporters' comments.

Other frequently used structures

- questions and answers, particularly when there is a lot of complex information to put across, for example with pensions
- chronology, particularly where the subject is a past or future event

Important principles

Hierarchy

Within these structures, your editing may involve you in deciding which points should come first within the structure, and which later. For example, in the Comparative structure (p. 43), should the text deal first with plot, theme, or character?

When deciding this, you should bear in mind that we expect information to be presented hierarchically—that is, we expect the most important or interesting points to appear first, and less important information to appear later in the document. So your really good or surprising ideas should appear early in the text.

Most important or interesting

Least important or interesting

The best order for your reader

The order should be the one that is best for your reader, not for you. Though you may have considered a subject under three separate headings, your reader may think differently. If that's the case, order the text the way they think and work, rather than the way you think and work.

Your projects   **Your chosen structure**

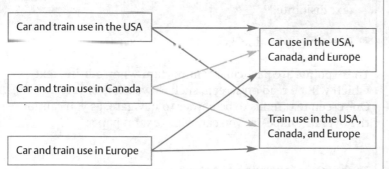

Do!

always keep a clean copy of the original text, on paper or on your system so that:

- you can check what the writer originally said

- if the paper copy gets messy, you can start afresh

- all is not lost if the system fails.

How to go about it

Structural changes can be quite drastic, so always keep a copy of the original on your system, on disk or paper, so that you can refer back to it.

As you consider structural flow, read through the text and ask yourself some fundamental questions.

- Which part of this information is likely to be the most important or interesting to my reader?

- Does the reader need certain points before others?

- If it's for reference, should I consider putting it in a footnote, endnote, or appendix?

- Could I present any information differently, for example by boxed text on the same page?

- Would cross-referencing make the text easier to follow?

- Should some parts of the text be divided into smaller sections?

- Are there too many sections and subdivisions, making the text disjointed?

- Does the 'story-line' keep moving forward?

These points are particularly important when editing text which will be read on screen, such as websites or intranet sites. On-screen text tends to be harder to navigate, as you cannot see the overall 'shape', as you can with text on paper.

Techniques for trying out structures

There are several techniques for experimenting with structures, which you might like to try. They are all methods of breaking the text down in order to build it up again.

Editing on screen

When editing on screen your system's software may help you.

An 'outliner' shrinks the text that you see on screen to head-ings only. This allows you to view the document's overall structure and to experiment with different structures by alter-ing the order of the headings, with the text moving 'invisibly' at the same time. When you select your preferred structure, the system will fill in the 'missing' text.

Use the colour highlighter to mark sections of text which seem to belong together, using different colours for different sec-tions if you want.

Editing on paper

If text needs drastic restructuring, before you can start work you may need to break it down into a diagrammatic form to find its overall shape. When you can see all the content on one page it is easier to reorganize it.

The charts on the preceding pages will help you draw out themes, shapes, and patterns. They will help you to identify whether there is a structure which simply needs emphasizing linguistically, or whether the text needs reshaping.

You may want to break the information down onto index cards, with headings and sub-headings. You can then experiment with laying these out in different ways to find the order which best suits the document's purpose.

Remember that once you change the structure and content of a document, the effects are likely to be far-reaching and could cause ripples of change throughout the whole document.

Best of both worlds

Remember you can move between paper and screen editing.

See Ch. 14, How technology can help you

Watch out!
Even small changes to the structure can prompt other changes to text. Be sure to check:

- cross-references, including those in the text
- page numbers
- section numbers
- diagram numbers
- placing of definitions and explanations.

8 Achieving linguistic flow

When editing, you will need to check that the text flows from section to section, that there are no jumps in the logic, and that the document hangs together. You also need to make sure that the *language* flows from word to word, sentence to sentence, and paragraph to paragraph. This is 'linguistic flow'.

Flowing from word to word

See Ch. 7, Achieving structural flow

Each word needs to fall into the most natural place in the sentence so that you can read the text aloud without it sounding clumsy or artificial. If a word does draw attention to itself, it should only be because you want it to.

See Ch. 12, Clarity

For example, in that last sentence the emphasis falls on 'does' and 'only'. Both words could be omitted, with little change to the rest of the sentence. You could make the emphasis more strong by moving 'only' to earlier in the sentence. A word should only draw attention to itself if you want it to.

Readers are likely to find the word order we use when we speak the easiest to understand. Read the text aloud, or 'hear' it in your head, to notice where the word order is awkward.

Achieving a natural word order may sometimes mean 'breaking' some of the so-called conventions of grammar and usage. It is acceptable to start sentences with 'and' or 'but', to split infinitives, or to end a sentence with a preposition if that is the best way to make the sense clear. Readers should be able to concentrate on *what* they are reading, not *how* it is written.

Read text aloud

Here is an example of an awkward sentence from an essay about education.

> By providing opportunities for women without professional qualifications, evening classes enabled them to participate in education and development without disruption to their domestic lives.

Quick tips:
Start with the subject.
Follow the thought through.
Read the text aloud.

This sentence suffers for the following reasons:

- It does not start with the subject (evening classes).

- It does not follow a direct route through the writer's main thought, which is 'evening classes enabled women to participate in education'.

- The use of the pronoun (them) is confusing, as it is preceded by four plural words (opportunities, women, qualifications, classes). This forces the reader to hesitate over which of these 'them' refers to.

With changes, the sentence flows more freely:

 Do!

use pronouns when they help to show how thoughts and ideas are linked.

> Evening classes enabled women who did not have professional qualifications to participate in education and development, without disrupting their domestic lives.

 Don't!

use them when they could cause confusion.

This example is from a company report:

> A factor which differentiates successful organizations is the ability to put to strategic use the research which they commission.

See Ch. 12, Clarity

This sentence appears clumsy because the reader is thrown by the phrase 'to put to strategic'. This is because, after 'the ability to' , the reader expects a simple verb, and gets an adjective and a noun. Some rewording would make it flow more smoothly:

> Successful organizations are differentiated by their ability to make strategic use of the research which they commission.

Flowing from sentence to sentence

Readers need to be able follow what is going on in the writer's mind as the writer's thoughts move from one idea to the next. By using 'linking' techniques you can help your readers to do this. When sentences are linked to each other, readers have to work less hard. They are also less likely to need to read passages a second time to grasp the meaning.

See Ch. 11, Brevity

The key to linking sentences, and paragraphs, is clear thinking. When editing text you wrote yourself, you will understand how your thoughts are connected. It's important to make sure that you demonstrate that connection, and that you are not tempted to edit out the connecting words because you need to be brief. If you are working on others' text, it can be harder to show the connections because you need to fully understand the writer's thought processes. If in doubt, ask.

Best tip for writer–editors
The more clearly you think, the more clearly you'll write.

The techniques

Refer back using pronouns

A pronoun is a word which stands in the place of a noun, such as 'it', 'they', 'those'. The connection between the following two facts becomes visible when a pronoun is used, instead of 'and'.

Quick tips for flowing text

- Use pronouns to refer back. They really work.

- Repeat a word from the previous sentence. Repeated words are easy to use.

- Show how your thoughts are connected. However, first you have to think clearly!

> The system was out of action for two hours and our customers experienced problems.

> The system was out of action for two hours <u>which</u> caused problems for our customers.

> John will be showing his paintings at the gallery in March. John's paintings are colourful abstracts and are popular with the gallery's customers.

> John will be showing his paintings at the gallery in March. <u>They</u> are colourful abstracts <u>which</u> are popular with <u>our</u> customers.

Refer back using 'so' and 'such'

> The system was out of action for two hours. We expected it would remain <u>so</u> for longer.

> John will be showing his colourful abstracts at the gallery in March.
> <u>Such</u> works are popular with our gallery's customers.

See Part B for words to help you 'flow'

Expose your thoughts

Show your reader how the ideas in one sentence are connected to those in the previous one.

When you are adding, explaining, reinforcing, try:

■ This explains why ...

■ In addition ...

■ Therefore ...

When you are introducing a new idea, or showing that your thoughts have moved on, try:

■ On the other hand ...

■ However ...

■ Alternatively ...

Let the words echo

A simple way of showing the connection is to echo a key word from the previous sentence:

> The system was out of action for two hours, which caused problems for our customers. These <u>problems</u> led to dozens of letters of complaint.

Flowing from paragraph to paragraph

Most written documents have more than one paragraph. The technique for showing how the paragraphs are connected is similar to that for linking sentences. However, because you or the writer will have begun a new paragraph to indicate a fairly significant change of subject or angle, the 'thought space' between paragraphs is usually larger than that between sentences. Therefore, you will often need to use a stronger phrase, or *transition*, to show the link.

There are two places where you can create flow between paragraphs. You can either link back to the preceding paragraph or link ahead to the following paragraph.

At the start of paragraphs

At the start of a paragraph you can link back to the preceding paragraph by using strong connecting words and phrases.

- This ... (followed by repetition of a word from the end of the previous paragraph)

- Another example ...

- I will now deal with ...

Use topic sentences

A transition can also pull the reader in by using a 'topic sentence'—one which tells the reader what the rest of the paragraph is going to be about.

> Safety on the sports field is an important issue for our club.

You can create topic sentences by implying questions 'who—what—when—where—why—how', and then answering it.

The following examples are from an article about redundancy.

> The biggest change could be in the size of your pay-off.
> (The rest of the paragraph explains the trend.)

> If your employer offers you a deal close to the statutory minimum, you have one very powerful tool at your disposal. (The rest of the paragraph explains what people can do under these circumstances.)

At the ends of paragraphs

Similarly, a transition at the end of a paragraph can hint at what the next paragraph will be about. The following examples are from a newspaper article about spies.

> He was a spy, not out of political conviction, not out of greed, but for the sheer romance of it. (The following paragraph goes into detail about why spying is often considered romantic.)

> He is called the 'unheralded superstar of international espionage'. (The following paragraph deals with the characters in films and novels about spying.)

This is how the same techniques might work in an essay:

> By comparing these two works we can identify some of the ways in which the novel has developed. (The following paragraph begins the comparison.)

A final example, this time from a company report:

> Many companies are concerned about the implications of instituting a knowledge management system. (The following paragraph explains what these concerns are, and attempts to expel them.)

Tip
Learn from others. When you read something which is easier to understand than you expected, look at the writer's use of transitions, to see how they have 'helped' you through the text.

9 Editing style and tone

See Ch. 10, Accuracy Ch. 3, Readers and Aims, Ch. 12, Clarity, and relevant Checklists in Part B

What is style?

When you edit the *accuracy* of a piece of text, you identify what is wrong with it. You could have to correct facts, figures, spelling, grammar, or punctuation. When you edit the *style*, you choose from a number of different ways of expressing the same thing. The decision you make will depend on your audience and your purpose.

We all have our own writing style, which is a combination of written characteristics such as our preferred sentence length, sentence complexity, and the words we prefer to use. Therefore, editors who work on others' text should be cautious about changing the style of the original piece of work, and only make stylistic changes if they are really necessary. That means when the original is:

■ unclear, because of sentence structure or length, or the vocabulary used;

■ inappropriate for the reader, or for the text's purpose.

Style is closely related to the tone of voice which comes across in a piece of writing. Getting that right can be difficult, because different people often 'hear' a different tone of voice in a piece of writing. It is also related to clarity, which is discussed in Chapter 12.

Know what's expected

Text is becoming less formal. Even organizations which used to be considered straitlaced are using a more relaxed style. However, some people or organizations are reluctant to adopt certain features of this more informal style. This may be part of the way an organization or person wants to present themselves—they may have chosen either to be friendly, or more distant. Sometimes, however, people are reluctant to change because they think a piece of writing cannot be both friendly and professional. Of course it can be, just as a person can be both friendly and professional.

See Ch. 4, Style guides

Although it only makes sense to use a formal style when you want a distant relationship with the reader, if your organization has conventions—a house style—follow their guidelines. Your editing job will be easier because many decisions about preferred alternatives have already been made.

See Part B on Style guides and Style guide checklist

✔ **Do!**

find out if there is a style you should follow, and keep to it.

Different texts, different tones

Not all text needs a friendly tone. Communications sometimes need to be firm or insistent, such as letters which instruct someone to pay an outstanding bill or follow a safety procedure. Your tone needs to be appropriate for the text, and the message. It should always be professional.

Communication	Formality rating
Contracts and legal correspondence	High
Job applications	Medium to high
Invitations	High or low
Personal letters	Low
Business letters and minutes	Medium to high
Essays	Medium to high
Theses, dissertations, academic text	High
E-mails and memos	Medium to low
Club newsletters	Low

What will influence the style you choose?

See Ch. 3 on
Readers and aims

The style you choose will be influenced by:

■ the level of formality you wish to adopt;

■ your knowledge of the reader;

■ the overall aims of a publication;

*Always keep to
the conventions
of your
organization or
style when you
are editing.*

■ the specific aims of the piece of text you are editing;

■ the type of text you are editing.

Once you are confident about these points, you can think about your text as having a place on a grid.

Know the reader well

Formal text ———————————————— Informal text

Don't know the reader at all

Note
You will want to be informal with people you know well. A manager dealing with someone whose work is below standard, or a club secretary telling people to obey club rules, would use a more formal tone.

You would place the text you are writing high up the vertical line if you know the reader well, and low down if you do not know them at all. Similarly, you would place the text to the left of the horizontal line if you are editing a traditionally formal document, such as a thesis, but to the right for an informal text, such as a club newsletter. The 'X' above is where you would position a memo to your boss; the 'O' above is where you might position a report to your managing director. Most communications fall within one of the shaded areas.

The ability to see your text on a grid can help you to see whether you should edit the text to make it more, or less, formal.

Many academics use very long sentences and almost unheard of words (epiphanic, metonymic). Some of them seem to enjoy making up words of their own (affectivity, pastness), and as a student, you've probably read books with page-long paragraphs. You may want to bear this 'academic style' in mind with your own word choice, sentence length, and paragraph length. But remember, different tutors will have different preferences.

How to make the tone less formal

If you are editing a sales letter, a memo to your boss, or a club newsletter, rather than wanting a formal tone, you will probably want to sound relaxed and friendly. A different type of document, such as a job application or a report, will probably need a more formal tone.

Note
You can be both informal and professional.

Something odd often happens when people write: they may start using words and sentence structures which they would never normally use, so that the text ends up sounding nothing like the person who wrote it. People seem to find it more difficult to write in a relaxed and informal style.

See Ch. 12, Clarity.

This can create difficulties for individuals and organizations. Text which is written in a rather formal manner is often more difficult to understand. It also gives the impression that a company or club is not a very friendly place; it's not really concerned about its customers or members. So, if you want people to understand what they are reading, and you want them to react in a reasonable and positive way, you should aim for a friendly, rather than formal, tone.

Note
People are more likely to react in a positive way if the tone is friendly, rather than formal.

Making the tone less formal can be tricky if you wrote the text yourself, but there are a number techniques you can try.

| ## Use 'you' or 'your'

The clever fact about using 'you' and 'your' in writing is that readers rarely notice how frequently the words are used. A recent one-page sales letter from a chain of department stores uses the words 26 times. Most readers simply comment that the letter seems helpful and personal. The technique can be applied even to really short communications.

> Members should not park their cars in front of the community centre when using the gym.

> Please do not park <u>your</u> car in front of the community centre when <u>you</u> are using the gym.

Use 'I' and 'we'

If you edit a document so that you use the words 'I' and 'we' you will create a piece with natural tone. The following examples progress from formal to informal.

The company has received your recent letter.

We have received your recent letter.

I have received your recent letter.

I've received your recent letter.

Note
Mixing 'I' and 'we' makes sense: it's what we do when we talk, and you can do it in writing too.

Mixing is fine

It's worth adding that you can mix 'I' and 'we' in a business letter, and it often makes sense to do so. Use 'I' when dealing with what you have done: 'I've checked the details …' and 'we' when writing about the organization: 'and confirm that we will be able to supply the forms by the end of the month'.

Avoid using 'I' too often

If the word 'I' appears too frequently in a piece, edit some of them out, particularly if lots of sentences start with 'I'. The following example makes the writer sound self-important; not an ideal impression to create when applying for a job.

> I saw your advertisement in last week's Evening Mercury and I believe I have many of the qualities you are seeking.
>
> I therefore have pleasure in enclosing a copy of my CV in which I set out details of the experience I have had in your industry.

Minor changes will make the letter sounds more natural, but still professional.

> I saw your advertisement in last week's Evening Mercury and believe I have many of the qualities you are seeking.
>
> Therefore, I have pleasure in enclosing a copy of my CV giving details of my experience in your industry.

Avoid replacing 'I' with 'myself'

Only use 'myself' and 'yourself' to emphasize the person you are referring to. The examples below sound self-effacing.

> Please return the form to myself by Friday.
>
> David or yourself should visit the Miami office, though you could ask Ann to go.

The correct use, in similar sentences, would be:

> Please return the form to me so that I can deal with it myself.
>
> David or you should visit the Miami office, but if you can't go yourself you could ask Ann.

Use contractions

Many organizations avoid contractions, even when they don't need to. This internal memo sounds rather formal.

> As the suppliers have not yet let us have their full costings we are not able to provide all the details at the moment. However, we will have all the information by the end of next week and I will contact you then.

This sounds more friendly.

> As the suppliers haven't yet let us have their full costings we're not able to provide all the details at the moment, but we'll have all the information by the end of next week. I'll contact you then.

Use everyday vocabulary

We will keep returning to this point in this book. Vocabulary is discussed in more detail in Chapter 12. Here it's worth considering types of words which often appear in writing.

Cut out the fashionable words

Be aware of modern jargon and fashionable words which may appear in the text you are editing. Words such as 'down-sizing', 'right-sizing', 'empowerment', and 'synergy' come into fashion and go out again.

- Ask what effect these words will have on the readers.

- Only use them if you are convinced the words will make readers take the document more seriously.

- Remember that what one person considers clever 'management-speak' another person will consider comic.

Some of the words which are best avoided (unless you are a law student)

- aforementioned
- hereafter
- hitherto
- hereinunder
- notwithstanding
- pursuant to
- undersigned

See Ch. 12, Clarity, for more words to avoid

Jump on jargon

Jargon is the special language which we need to use to get through our working day. It's a kind of verbal shorthand. All jobs and professions have jargon and so do clubs, companies, and individual departments within companies. Sometimes this might be just initials, such as ISA for independent savings account or NQT for newly qualified teacher.

Alternatively, jargon can be words such as when the insurance industry writes of 'captives' (a way of managing insurance) or printers write about 'gutters' (the space on the page either side of the binding). Words only really become 'jargon' when they are used outside the group who are 'in the know'.

When people do not know the jargon they may:

■ feel excluded by the writer;

■ stop reading;

■ not understand the text;

■ guess at the meaning, and guess wrongly;

■ waste your time by telephoning to ask what you mean;

■ get the wrong impression of the writer.

When editing, think carefully about *all* the people who are likely to read what you are editing. If any of them may not be familiar with the words you are using, you should either:

■ choose a different word, or

■ explain the jargon, or

■ provide a list which defines the jargon.

Avoid pompous phrases and Latin

Today we would laugh, or be puzzled, if a letter began 'Thank you for your letter of the 30th ult.' and ended 'I remain your obedient servant'. Yet these phrases were once the normal way of beginning and ending business letters. 'Ult.' was used until about 25 years ago, and meant 'last month'. We now communicate more naturally.

Part of an editor's job could involve removing outdated phrases such as 'hereinunder' and 'hitherto', which are often used just to impress, or to pad out a document.

It is also a good idea to edit out any Latin phrases which have crept in. Phrases such as *pro tem*, *seriatim*, and *sine qua non* are usually there to impress. Readers often feel intimidated when language is used this way, or they laugh.

When Latin is allowed

There are a few exceptions to the overall advice about avoiding Latin. If you are involved in editing minutes for a committee which is run very formally, the members and the chair may use Latin as part of the procedures. When this happens, it is normal to use the same phrases in the minutes. You should put the word or words in *italics*.

Another exception is if you work in certain professions, or are studying particular subjects, such as law or medicine.

As always, be aware of the conventions of your organization, subject, and the type of text you are editing.

Gardeners need not weed it out

Gardeners are another group of people who may find life easier if they use some Latin. The names of plants vary from country to country, and even from area to area. So, if you live abroad and want to create a romantic English garden of Forget-me-nots, Honesty, and Love-in-a-mist, you will be more likely to find what you are looking for if you ask for *Myosotis*, *Lunaria*, and *Nigella*.

How to create a firm or formal tone

■ Formalize the tone by using slightly longer sentences than usual. But remember that sentences more than 25 to 30 words long can be difficult to understand.

■ Use very short sentences when you want to be firm. 'This account is now overdue.'

■ Choose more complex words. 'This has caused extra work for our department' becomes 'This has necessitated additional work for our department'.

■ Use more complex sentence structures. 'I understand' becomes 'It is my understanding that…'

■ Put negatives in full. 'We can't accept this delay' becomes 'We cannot accept this delay'.

■ Number the points you are making: 'firstly … secondly … thirdly … finally …'

■ Use repetition: 'We have … we have … we have also … '; or, 'even if … even if … .'

■ Omit softening phrases. 'As you are aware …' becomes 'As you know …'.

■ Do not flinch at using strong words. 'You should …' becomes 'You must …'.

■ Do not be afraid to call a spade a spade. 'Although you said you were paying, the cheque appears not to have been enclosed' becomes 'Despite your undertaking to pay, the cheque was not enclosed'.

■ Create distance between the writer and the reader. 'As you know …' becomes 'Readers will be aware …'.

■ Long documents tend to appear more formal than short ones.

Strong words and phrases for action

… you must …

… we will not allow …

… without delay …

… I consider …

… I want …

… I insist …

… have to …

… it is essential that …

… it is necessarry to …

Strong words and phrases for feelings

I am …

… shocked

… amazed

… dismayed

… appalled

… unable to understand why

10 Accuracy

Why accuracy matters

An important part of the role of a writer-editor and an editor is
to make sure that the finished document is completely accurate.
Any mistakes create a poor impression of the writer, editor,
department, and organization. When there are inaccuracies in a
document, readers will tend to distrust everything including the
statistics, the opinions and the facts. Students who do not spell
or punctuate correctly are often marked down for their mistakes.

Remember, a written document is like a shop window. It is
your way of showing members, customers, colleagues, or tutors
just how good you are.

Lots to do—and some doubtful helpers

'Accuracy' is an enormous area. It covers checking that the text
is factually and grammatically correct, as well as ensuring that
you and the writer have adhered to the style guidelines for the
document. That means the editor has a lot to think about.

Checking for accuracy is:

- highly detailed;

- time-consuming;

- painstaking.

However it is really worth taking the trouble to do
it carefully.

Technology and accuracy: help or hindrance?

Editors who use computers know how useful they are. Many people who work with text would be unhappy not to have an on-screen spelling checker. However, there are serious risks in relying on a grammar or spelling checker and assuming that all is well. A word processor would accept the following sentence, although four of the thirteen words are wrong in context and the sentence is nonsense.

> I have not received the completed from witch I will send you to revue.

> I have now received the completed form which I will send you to review.

Grammar checkers are similarly unreliable, as they suggest changes without explanations. This means that, if you adopt many of the suggested changes, you will change correct text to wrong text. Use them with caution, or not at all.

Watch out!
Never rely on a spelling or grammar checker to make your text accurate. They are useful—up to a point. But there are many mistakes they won't spot, and they cannot check that the word is correct in context.

See Ch. 14, How technology can help you, and Part B for style guides and checklists on accuracy, brevity, clarity, and style.

What needs to be accurate?

The short answer to that is 'everything', but you need to take special care with:

- names of people, places, organizations;

- numbers, dates, sections, page numbers;

- spelling—including words with more than one spelling;

- punctuation;

- grammar;

- consistency in punctuation, abbreviations, use of capitals.

How to go about it

You should check the *factual* accuracy of the text while you are editing the content. This chapter is concerned with the *linguistic* accuracy of the text. It makes sense to check the linguistic accuracy after all the other checking. If you look at the detail early on, you may check text which you'll later delete, or overlook new text which you have added.

With short documents, you can check the text in one or two steps. With longer documents you may want to check separately for each item, working section by section.

See Ch. 5, First steps

Many editors keep to the following sequence, but whether you follow this method or one of your own, make sure that you have a stepped approach for longer documents.

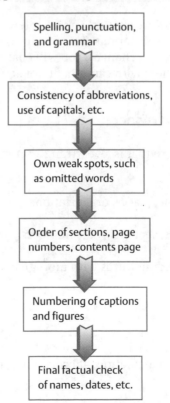

Spelling, punctuation, and grammar

Consistency of abbreviations, use of capitals, etc.

Own weak spots, such as omitted words

Order of sections, page numbers, contents page

Numbering of captions and figures

Final factual check of names, dates, etc.

Look out for ambiguities

It can be hard to see whether a piece of text you wrote yourself is ambiguous, because you know your intended meaning. Asking someone else to read your text is the most sure way of avoiding ambiguity. The following examples show some of the most frequent causes of ambiguity.

> Residents refuse to go in bins.

Missing apostrophes can make nonsense of a passage. Once the missing punctuation mark is used, the meaning is clear.

See Part B on editing a document as a team

> We must employ more highly skilled staff.

Here the confusion is caused by the use of 'more', which can apply to quality or quantity. The sentence needs to be amplified, or 'more' could be replaced with 'additional'.

See Ch 5. and Part B for more about style guides

See Part B for checklists

> Two years for terrifying pensioner.

Headlines are so brief that they are often misleading. Here the sentence has no subject, and no verb. As a result we're uncertain whether the pensioner was terrifying or terrified.

> Tickets are available for the soccer game in reception.

Here, the confusion is caused by sentence structure. The information 'in reception' is too far from the adverb 'available'. Put them back together for a sensible sentence.

> People used to visit the city to see how poor it was; now they go there to see what can be done.

The meaning intended was 'to see what has been achieved'. It is confusing because the phrase 'can be done' is in the present but is being used to express the past.

Know your weaknesses

Everyone has mistakes they frequently make, and points they frequently miss, both at the writing and at the editing stage of creating a document. It's worth getting to know the mistakes you commonly make, and the details you miss when you are checking a document.

■ Do a special check for points you often overlook.

■ If your computer software includes 'auto-correct', you can set it up to correct your most frequent mistakes automatically.

■ If you edit text written by someone else, try to become familiar with the errors they tend to make.

Work as a team

When you are part of a team, try to get to know which parts of editing your colleagues are good at, and where your own strengths are. If you work on text as a team you will be able to correct each other's mistakes and ambiguities.

Create and use a style guide

Create a style guide, on paper or on screen, to give answers to accuracy questions which occur frequently.

Use checklists

Checklists save time by reminding you of the points that you need to look for when you are editing for accuracy. There are a number of checklists in Section B, but by creating your own you will have reminders which are specific to the kind of work you do.

Proof checking

After your final edit, you will need to check the completed text. This is your final opportunity to correct mistakes and omissions. Proof checking means correcting what is wrong, rather than choosing to express an idea differently.

At this stage it is unusual to add text or make large deletions. Depending on how the text is to be produced, late changes by the editor, rather than corrections, can be expensive as well as time-consuming. Therefore, you should deal with such changes earlier in the editing process.

Some professional tricks

Many professional checkers make one of their 'reads' of the text 'backwards', from the last word through to the first, to help them to check each word separately. It is slow to do, but does help you spot spelling and typographical errors.

Also, as you will always be more fresh when you start proof checking than when you finish, with long documents it's worth making one of your checks from the last page through to the first. That way, you may spot more errors.

Proof-checking traditions

If someone else, such as a printer or typist, will make the changes for you, it's important to make sure that the changes you want to be carried out are very clear. When you are proof-checking text, it is traditional to:

- mark the text both in the line and in the margin;

- use red pen, or another highly visible colour;

- use standard proof-checking symbols.

Proof-checking list

Spelling and grammar

⬇

Consistency

⬇

Weak spots

⬇

Ordering

⬇

Numbering

⬇

Final check of facts

⎭ insert

� delete

≢ change to lower case

= change to caps

〜〜 change to bold

⊔ change to italics

See Part B for proof-checking symbols

11 | Brevity

It is a fact of modern life that most people prefer to read a short document rather than a long one. In their working and private lives people are pressed for time, and a long piece of text can look daunting to read. Such documents are often put to one side, to be read later. Some recipients may never read them, relying on others to keep them up to date if the content is important.

As with all editing, when trying to shorten a piece of text, always consider your reader and the document's purpose.

There are other important points concerning brevity.

When brief is not best

See Ch. 3, Readers and aims

While most people prefer a short document, sometimes producing a short piece of text may not be the best idea.

- When consultants carry out research and produce reports, their clients usually like substantial documents.

- Tutors who ask for a 5,000-word essay want 5,000 words, not 2,000.

- Complex or technical subjects often need explaining at length, which may make it impracticable to aim for a document which is brief.

Brief and clear are not the same

Brief and clear are not the same, and do not necessarily go together. A piece of text could be brief, but not at all clear.

> HR's OHP with R&D for TMs 1.7–3.7.

See Ch. 12, Clarity

If you follow the guidelines on clarity in Chapter 12, your text may become slightly longer. This is because the way you structure sentences to make them clear often involves adding explanatory and 'helping' words. So, although the individual words may be shorter, the edited text can be longer than the 'unclear' version.

The two ways to be brief

There are two ways you can be brief with a piece of text.

Watch out!
Just what does this message mean?

Heating not working. Jones responsible. Hasn't worked since 1.12.

- Make sure all the content is relevant .

- Use language as concisely as possible.

Keep the content brief

See Ch. 3, Readers and aims

Often, text can be made more brief by deleting some of the information it contains, always with the reader and the purpose of the document in mind. Questions you should ask yourself when considering whether you can delete some of the content as part of your editing are dealt with in Chapter 6, Editing the content.

See Ch. 6, Editing the content

It's worth noting that you may be able to make the overall document more brief by adding to it!

Being brief with language

See Part B for
Brevity checklist

Cut out rambling

Rambling is wandering. It's what sometimes happens when people enjoy writing: the words tumble out but take too long to get anywhere.

When editing, delete any rambling, which is often accompanied by long sentences.

> With reference to the memo I received from you concerning a proposed change to our existing pay system I have conducted a preliminary investigation into the feasibility of the company adopting a credit transfer system.

The text should either:

Tip
Aim to take the
"motorway" route
through the ideas,
not a pretty detour.

■ make the point and reinforce it, or

■ present information which leads to the point, or

■ increase enjoyment or understanding with descriptions.

When you wonder where the words are taking you, there's a chance that the writer has rambled. Cut out irrelevancies and asides so that readers can 'walk' through the text, rather than wander.

Look for wasted words

As writers, when words fall into place easily we are reluctant to stop writing. Unfortunately, that's often when unnecessary, wasted words creep in. A wasted word is one that is not playing an essential role in the sentence. Editing is a chance to remove these words, and to check that every phrase and word you have chosen helps to make the meaning clear.

> Although these may sound like very small amendments which only allow you to cut out an odd word here and there, even in one short sentence the changes can make your text considerably shorter.

> ~~Although~~ these ~~may~~ sound like ~~very~~ small amendments which only ~~allow you to~~ cut out ~~an~~ odd word ~~here and there,~~ ~~even in one short sentence~~ the changes can make your text considerably shorter.

Lᴛ
Lˢ   Lyet

Most people find it easier to see the wasted words in others' work than in their own, but with practice it does become easier. Writer-editors gradually learn which of the words and structures they use are unnecessary, and start to change them at the writing stage.

Meanwhile, there are ways to improve your skill at finding wasted words.

- The following pages give examples of language habits which cause text to be over-long, and show you how to shorten the text.

- You can also practise by calling up a piece of text onto your screen and seeing how much you can delete without changing the sense.

Tip
Call up a piece of text onto your screen and see how much you can cut without changing the meaning.

Look out for two-part verbs

Try using a simple verb instead of a verb made up of two parts. This will slightly change the meaning, but the change will not matter in many contexts.

Avoid this	Prefer this
The company is spending	The company spends
I am enclosing	I enclose
I work as a secretary	I am a secretary

Use single words to replace a phrase

You can often replace a phrase with a single word:

on the subject of ——————→	about *or* concerning
in order to ——————→	to
the process of consultation ➤	consultation

In practice this can lead to text that is 30 per cent shorter.

Tip
If you're a writer-editor, think about these points while you're writing. You will save a lot of time.

> I know my colleague has written to you on the subject of our meeting and am now enclosing the relevant forms in order to allow the process of consultation to begin. (31 words)

⬇

> I know my colleague wrote to you about our meeting and I enclose the relevant forms to allow consultation to begin. (21 words)

The following extract from a report looks back on a meeting. By omitting wasted words and using single words to replace phrases, you can reduce it by almost half.

L and give

> Our brief was to organize a symposium on the subject ~~to be held~~ in London at which the managers were to ~~be given the chance of could~~ discuss~~ing the treatment of~~ the new legislation, ~~and to allow us to obtain~~ an overall view ~~as to the extent~~ of any problems, and ~~together with any~~ possible solutions. ~~that were apparent to them~~

As well as reducing the text from 61 words to 32 words, the edited version is easier to follow.

> Our brief was to organize a symposium on the subject in London, at which the managers were to discuss the new legislation and give an overall view of problems and possible solutions.

Delete unnecessary, lazy, or inelegant repetition

There are different types of repetition.

Stylistically, repetition can be very effective. 'An outstanding club, with outstanding players' emphasizes the quality of both the club and the players. This is 'elegant repetition', a stylistic device which you can use—sparingly—in your text.

However, sometimes a word is used twice in a short space because of laziness. The result is inelegant, rather than stylish, as in 'The director considered her application and considered she would make a good manager'. It would be better to change one use of 'considered' to 'thought' or 'believed'.

Be aware of unnecessary repetition, or 'tautology', such as:

'combined together'—things cannot be combined separately

'reverted back'—you cannot revert forward

'true facts'—there is no such thing as untrue fact.

More can be less

Although it seems like a contradiction, you can make your overall document more brief by adding to it.

- Cross referencing will prevent you having to repeat information in different places.

- Abbreviations and acronyms such as OHP help to keep text short. Put the words in full the first time they are used, with the abbreviation in a bracket: overhead projector (OHP). From then on, use just the abbreviation. A list of all abbreviations you are using is also helpful.

- Placing some of the detail in footnotes, appendices, or endnotes will enable you to provide the information while making the document seem less bulky.

> *Surprise!*
> You may be able to make your overall document shorter, by adding to it!

Beware of over-editing

Sometimes editors work so hard at making the text brief that they over-edit and delete so much text that the meaning becomes harder, rather than easier, to understand. This is because many of the transitions and 'helping words' are cut out, as in this extract from an article on training in an in-flight magazine.

> Instead of ticking hundreds of boxes to demonstrate certain procedures have been followed, companies will have to convince assessors that training initiatives have helped meet business goals.

Just five extra words would make the meaning more clear.

ʟthat

ʟthe ʟthem to ʟtheir

> Instead of ticking hundreds of boxes to demonstrate certain procedures have been followed, companies will have to convince assessors that training initiatives have helped meet business goals.

> Thanks to the turnaround of people's thinking, causes you thought lost can be revived.

This sentence is confusing because, on first reading, you are uncertain whether 'causes' is a verb or a noun. In fact, in this sentence it's a noun. If the editor had put in a 'that' the meaning would have been clear immediately.

> Thanks to the turnaround of people's thinking, causes that you thought were lost can be revived.

> The unit was not sealed and liable to flooding.

See Ch. 10, Accuracy, for more about ambiguity

This sentence from an accident report is ambiguous because it has been over-edited. It could mean that the unit was not sealed *and not* liable to flooding, or that the unit was not sealed and *therefore* it *was* liable to flooding. This is better.

> As the unit was not sealed it was liable to flooding.

Précis

A précis is a summary of a passage which maintains the order and proportions of the original, and gives its full sense. It has the content and balance of the original, and no new information is added. It is completely true to the original, but often about one-third of its length. A good précis reads like a piece of original writing.

Editors who have to précis passages are rewriting, rather than editing.

The technique is as follows:

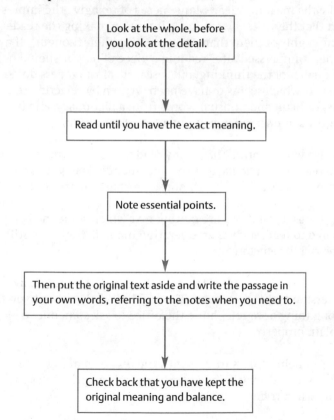

Look at the whole, before you look at the detail.

Read until you have the exact meaning.

Note essential points.

Then put the original text aside and write the passage in your own words, referring to the notes when you need to.

Check back that you have kept the original meaning and balance.

12 | Clarity

Note:
Aim to express the
meaning, not to
impress the reader.

See Ch. 7 on
structural flow and
Ch. 8 on linguistic
flow

Make the text say what it means

When you are editing, one of your primary aims should be to make the meaning clear. Many pieces of text give the impression that the writers were more intent on making the reader think highly of them than on expressing their thoughts. If a reader is impressed after reading a piece of text, it should be by the quality of the thinking and research. Most readers do not like text which seems to have been written by selecting the most difficult and unusual words from a dictionary, and by lengthy sentences which are whole paragraphs long.

It's also worth noting that many readers will find an excuse to stop reading, particularly if the document is one which they haven't requested, such as a house journal that arrives on employees' desks each month, or a letter from a company selling things. Even if you are editing text which someone is obliged to read, such as an operating manual, they may still approach it reluctantly.

Worst of all, if the text is too complex, readers simply may not understand what you mean. They will be likely either to do the wrong thing or to telephone the office to ask someone to explain properly.

You can help readers to stay with the text by making sure that it flows, but also by being clear. There are six principles to apply when trying to make a piece of text clear.

Important changes to make

The three most important guidelines deal with:

- using the most everyday word you can;

- keeping sentences short;

- keeping sentences simple. This is the most complex of these guidelines, and includes several different ideas.

> If the subject of the text is complicated, it's even more important to edit for clarity.

Before starting to think about these guidelines, let's take a look at a passage which doesn't follow them. It's an extract from a long club newsletter. It is perfectly correct, but it is written in an old-fashioned and rather pompous way.

> Members should understand that the granting of privileges by the Club diminishes the potential income from the shop and from entry charges, especially the latter, since hitherto the very modest subscription has also allowed free entry to a guest. It has become increasingly clear that the amount of financial support given to the Club by the members has not been commensurate with the benefits conferred on members.

Use the most everyday word you can

No two words have exactly the same meaning. There are, for example, dozens of different alternatives to the word 'understand'. They include 'appreciate', 'digest', 'follow', 'interpret', 'read', 'surmise', 'comprehend', and 'deduce'. The editor's job is to spot those words which are not doing the job they are intended to do.

Felix catus reclined on the kilim

How do you decide which to use?

When choosing which word to use, consider:

See Part B: The editor's toolkit

- all the possible meanings of the word in the original text;

- all the possible alternative words, using your thesaurus and your dictionary to help you;

- who the reader is;

See Ch. 3, Readers and aims

- the type of text you are editing;

- the purpose of the text.

Then ask yourself an important question.

> Would I lose my essential meaning by using a more simple word?

When deciding, remember that words change their meaning in context. Just a few meanings of the word 'simple' are:

simple →
- artless, when used of a poem
- elementary, when used of an exam or test
- informal, when used of a meal
- stark, when used of a monk's cell
- pure, when used of cosmetics
- unadorned, when used of a diagram

> It has become increasingly clear that the amount of financial support given to the Club by the members has not been commensurate with the benefits conferred on members.

Both 'commensurate' and 'conferred' are quite unusual words. Instead of 'commensurate with', the writer could have tried constructing the sentence to use 'in proportion to', or 'equal to'. 'Conferred' could be replaced with 'granted' or 'given to'.

> ... has not been in proportion to the benefits which members receive.

Avoiding weighty sentences

Of course, you can use the more difficult words too, and you should. If we never use them, they will disappear from our language, which would make our communications less subtle and less interesting.

Try thinking about the longer words as high-calorie snacks. Most of us can eat an occasional cream doughnut or éclair without problems, but we know we shouldn't eat a lot of them. If we do that we would have a stodgy diet, which would be difficult to digest. This is true of writing as well: use too many long words and the text becomes stodgy and difficult to digest. Remember to watch your reader's diet. You may be able to digest the more difficult words, but can your reader?

Keep sentences short

Some writers think long sentences are impressive; most readers dislike them. It can be harder to write short and clear sentences. As an editor you may often need to do something about the length of the sentences in the piece you are working on.

How long is short?

Short sentences are easier to understand. They are also easier to deal with as you don't get lost when you are reading. They are also easier to punctuate correctly.

You should aim for sentences with an average length of 15–20 words. The question is: how do you get from a long and rambling sentence to a number of short interesting ones?

A few tips should help.

■ Look for link words, such as 'and', 'but', 'who'. These are points where you could break the sentence.

■ Look for the idea the writer seemed to be trying to put across. If there are several in the sentence, separate them.

■ Try hearing the sentence in your head as you read it, and listen for when you would drop your voice.

The following passage is the closing sentence of letter from a food manufacturing company, in reply to a complaint letter. If the writer had tried out one of those ideas it would have read a lot better.

> Please be assured that the highest standards of hygiene and housekeeping are continually and rigorously enforced at all this company's premises and we would ask you to give our products another chance to show their normal high quality by using the enclosed vouchers which will be accepted by main stockists in exchange for any of our Nuts, Crisps, or Snacks of your choice.

That sentence contains three or four ideas. The addition of some full-stops makes it more clear and much more readable.

> Please be assured that the highest standards of hygiene and housekeeping are continually and rigorously enforced at all this company's premises. We would ask you to give our products another chance to show their normal high quality by using the enclosed vouchers. They will be accepted by main stockists in exchange for any of our Nuts, Crisps, or Snacks of your choice.

A warning for students

As a student you have probably noticed that academic writing can be rather different from other types of writing. You almost certainly know how hard it can be to follow the argument in long passages that seem to lose the thread part way through. You probably find you have to read some paragraphs several times before you can make sense of them.

Academic writing tends to have its own conventions, which often include:

- longer sentences

- long paragraphs

- more complex vocabulary

When you are being examined, the person reading your paper or essay may need to be sure that you have a wide vocabulary and can use language with more complex structures. There is sometimes a hint of 'writing to impress' about academic writing.

As a student, you should follow the conventions of academic writing. But, as with all types of writing, it all comes back to considering the reader. Notice which tutors seem to prefer a more 'traditional' academic style, and which are happy with a more straightforward style. Then, write the way they want you to write.

When you write long sentences, you will need to pay extra attention to the structure and shape of what you have written so that your meaning is still clear. The following section on sentence structure should help you.

| # Keep sentences simple

Often, editing involves taking sentences which are both long and extremely complicated, and making sense of them.

When editing someone else's work, you may have to read the sentence several times before you can make sense of it. You are doing that so that the reader will be able to understand it on just one reading. As you read through the sentence:

■ look for the thought;

■ look for non-essential information which has been added, such as descriptions, asides or definitions;

■ keep asking, 'What is this writer thinking?'

If you are editing your own work you know what the sentence means, which is why it's particularly important to try to leave a gap between writing and editing. Then, when you start to work on the piece, with each sentence or paragraph, ask yourself:

■ Does this section contain just one clear idea?

■ Have I expressed that idea as clearly as possible?

■ Can my reader follow the passage from start to end without getting lost?

This extract is from an assurance company's literature.

> Provided that there are no occupational, location or travel hazards present other than those which have been notified to us, that at least 80% of the eligible employees join the Plan at the outset, and that 80% of those employees who subsequently join the employer's service enter the Plan when first eligible, a No-Evidence Limit will normally be available for an amount as notified in each case.

That passage is almost impossible to understand after reading it just once, partly because you have to remember so much before you get to the point of the sentence. The extract needs a lot of editing, but just one change would make it more clear. This is what happens if you move the end of the sentence to the beginning and add some bullet points.

> A No-Evidence Limit will normally be available for an amount as notified in each case, provided that:
>
> ● there are no occupational, location or travel hazards present other than those which have been notified to us;
>
> ● at least 80% of the eligible employees join the Plan at the outset; and,
>
> ● 80% of those employees who subsequently join the employer's service enter the Plan when first eligible.

It is particularly important to edit documents for clarity if the subject being written about is complicated in the first place. This means complicated for the person it is intended for, not for the writer or editor. You have 'double trouble' if you add complicated language to a complicated subject.

The following sentence, from a student essay on A. S. Byatt's novel *Possession*, seems to have 'lost the will to live'. The reader is forced to go through it a second time to find the meaning, and may not be lucky even then.

> This description is the first time the action of the novel relocates to the past, rather than describing the past, bringing another strand to the book's structure by giving the readers knowledge of the actual past, to add to their knowledge of the present, the past as known through letters and diaries and the unknown past, and is one of only three such relocations (the others being the events surrounding Randolph's death, and the final chapter) and like the others makes us observers of intimate scenes.

Tip

Break the text up by using

● bullet points
● numbered points
● headings
● sub-headings
● diagrams and charts
● tabulations

As part of an academic essay, the sentence can afford to be quite long, but not 86 words of confusion. The writer needs to spend some time sorting out their thoughts:

> This description is the first time the action of the novel relocates to the past, as previously it only described the past. It thus brings another strand to the book's structure, and gives readers knowledge of the actual past. This supplements their knowledge of the present, of the past as known through letters and diaries, and of the unknown past. The novel relocates to the past only three times. The two other instances are when describing the events surrounding Randolph's death, and the final chapter. All three instances make the reader an observer of intimate scenes.

Writing and speaking have grown closer

When we speak we tend to express our thoughts quite simply.

During the last fifty years, the written English used by banks, governments, and other bodies has become closer to that used by people when speaking with respect to their intellectual equals. The change makes editing much easier.

When we speak we tend to express our thoughts quite simply. We say 'We went to a meeting' or 'The lecturer received your essay' or 'The novel was complex'.

The thoughts go in this order:

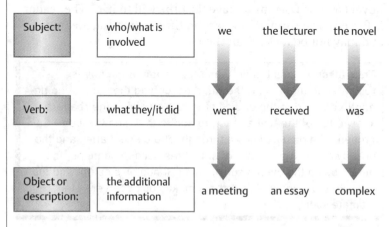

Subject:	who/what is involved	we	the lecturer	the novel
Verb:	what they/it did	went	received	was
Object or description:	the additional information	a meeting	an essay	complex

This applies not just to ideas which are in the past, as the examples are, but to anything in the present or future as well.

Writers often make their work over-complex by putting those ideas the other way round.

Object	Verb	Subject
The meeting	was attended	by us

To simplify this sentence you need to change the word order. Sometimes this may prompt other minor changes to the text.

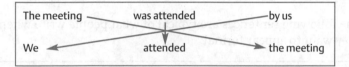

The grammar checker on computers sometimes comments that a writer has used the 'passive', and suggests using the 'active'. When it does this, it is suggesting that you order your thoughts as subject–verb–object/description.

The club newsletter example has two examples of the 'passive' word order: 'the granting of privileges by the club' could say 'when the club grants privileges'; 'the amount of financial support given to the club by the members' could say 'the amount of financial support which the members give the club'.

| **Putting these rules together**

We've done a lot of work on that one paragraph at the start of this chapter. Putting the ideas so far into practice, it reads like this:

> You may not realize that by granting privileges to members we reduce our income from the shop and from entry charges. Also, the subscription allows free entry for a guest. Increasingly, the amount of financial support which members give the Club is not in proportion to the benefits they receive.

People, not theories

The following sentences are typical of what people write when they want to appear formal:

> The fire alarms must be checked daily.
>
> It is understood that the goods will be delayed at customs.
>
> A management charge is made for looking after the account.

These sentences do not give a sense of anyone being involved in the action. Though they are grammatically correct, the sense of them is incomplete because they do not answer the question 'who?' Grammatically, this is known as an 'impersonal impassive'.

When readers do not have the 'who' part of a sentence, they may be confused, perplexed, or may guess wrongly at the missing answer.

Naming people avoids confusion

In the first example, it is not clear who should check the alarms. The sentence would be better if the writer answered the 'who' question, so that there was no doubt:

> The caretaker must check the fire alarms daily.

Naming people avoids curiosity

The second example also fails to answer the question 'who?' In this case a reader would be likely to ask, who says? customs? the export manager? or is the writer guessing because there were delays in the past? The sentence would be more clear if the editor answered the question 'who?'

> Our export manager has told me that the goods are likely to be delayed in customs.

Naming people can prevent irritation

In the third example, the readers will interpret the meaning of the sentence for themselves, possibly wrongly. In this case, they may assume that the company writing the letter is making the charge, though it may be made by a third party.

> The bank will charge you for looking after the account.

Tip
Use sentences that say who is doing what to avoid confusing readers, or leading them to guess the missing information.

Scientific writing has different conventions

Unlike other forms of writing, scientific writing is often written in this impersonal tense. If your editing is scientific, you should follow the convention.

In a thesis or scientific essay, the following structures would be preferred:

> The sample was weighed.
>
> The solution was heated to 50 degrees.
>
> Sodium is known to be highly reactive.

Be positive, not negative

There are two reasons for changing sentences to be written in a positive way, rather than a negative one.

■ A positive sentence is clearer and easier to understand.

■ It is better to tell people something positive than to tell them something negative.

The following sentences express a negative idea and could be edited to put the thoughts across in a more positive way. By telling readers what they should *not* do, this sentence forces them to work out for themselves what they *should* do.

> Never fail to back up your work at the end of the day.

If the editor makes a small change, the sense is more clear.

> Always back up your work at the end of the day.

Positive is easier to understand

Why tell people something negative?

If you were joining a club or society, the following letter might make you wonder how friendly the members were.

> We cannot enrol you as a member as you have not confirmed how you wish to pay your membership fee.

A simple change makes the members sound more friendly.

> We can enrol you as a member when you have confirmed how you wish to pay your membership fee.

Some negative sentences should be left that way, particularly if you are emphasizing the negative side of a situation, or something that should not be done.

> I have not received the information requested last month.
>
> You must not send your children to school if you think they are unwell.

These sentences are quite strong. Some of that strength is lost if they are expressed in a positive way.

> I am awaiting the information requested last month.
>
> You should only send your children to school if you are certain that they are well.

Prefer verbs to nouns

Text which uses a lot of verbs, rather than nouns, tends to be shorter and more clear, because it is closer to the way we speak.

> Commencement of the building work will be on 1 February.

> The building work will commence on 1 February.

Better still ...

> The building work will start on 1 February.

> When you have submitted your formal job application we will make arrangements for an interview.

> When you have formally applied for the job, we will arrange an interview.

Tip
Look out for nouns ending in '-tion'. Many of them lend themselves to being changed into verbs. When you do that, you'll have to change some other words too.

communication—
communicate

modification—
modify

motivation—
motivate

implementation—
implement

13 | Beyond ABC

Do!

consider making the text interesting by using some stylistic devices.

Don't!

trample on the author's feelings by changing the style.

See Part B on the 'editing contract'

Bring the text to life

Most editors invest a lot of time in making sure that the text:

- contains the right information;

- has an appropriate tone;

- flows well structurally;

- flows smoothly linguistically;

- is accurate;

- is brief;

- is clear.

You may also need to bring the text to life, to make it stand out or be more entertaining. This may be part of your role, but you should proceed with caution.

Who owns the text?

Your right to make changes depends on who 'owns' the text. You can change anything in your own work, but if someone else wrote the text, explain what you would like to change, and why. If you have a good reason, such as wanting to help the readers keep on reading, they may accept your idea. If the writer is unhappy about your suggestions, respect their wishes, particularly if the writer is the acknowledged or named author.

If the situation regarding changes becomes awkward, you will find it easier to deal with if you have an 'editing contract' which sets out the rights of the author and the editor.

More points to consider

■ If you are going to add any elegant touches, the rest of the text must be factually and linguistically perfect. If it is not, the special devices you have used will be lost—and may even be considered mistakes.

■ Any 'adornments' to the text will have most impact when the remainder of the text is in a plain style.

■ You must still have your readers and their needs firmly in mind. Though you may long to do something to make the text special, the person whose opinion matters most is the reader.

■ Keep within the constraints of your organization or discipline. In very traditional organizations, and in scientific and academic writing, the normal style is plain and unembellished. Any extra touches would normally be considered inappropriate.

What you can do

Use no-verb sentences for impact

Placed into a perfect piece of writing, these verb-free sentences would stand out, and be a powerful way of emphasizing the point. Of course, this only works if the rest of the text is grammatically conventional.

> So much for the environment.
>
> Not charity, not gifts—but work.
>
> So, a great success all round.

One of the most important aims of any editor is to be factually and linguistically perfect.

See Ch. 2 and Part B for working as part of a team and the 'editing contract'.

Use very long sentences to create atmosphere

Very long but carefully punctuated sentences can be used humorously or to enhance your description of someone who is very busy. Of course, this only works if you have the overall sentence length well under control. The following extract is from a humorous article about the stress of working on a newspaper:

> All this is on top of a caterwauling chorus of obscure pop songs from the art department, an intermittent hum from the 'novelty radio' on the editorial secretary's shelf, and a miscellaneous series of interruptions involving unpaid invoices, half-overheard conversations, and a James Bond look-alike who's been drafted in to add some vitality to the subbing team.

Use adjectives effectively

Some newspapers have almost banned the words 'key' and 'major' because they are so overused. English is a rich language, and you will make the text you edit more lively and interesting by changing these commonplace adjectives for something more specific.

By using a few adjectives carefully, you can change a piece of text from bland to vivid. Each of the following creates a different picture in the reader's mind:

> He was wearing a suit and drove a car.
>
> He was wearing a crumpled suit and drove a battered car.
>
> He was wearing an expensive new suit and drove a red sports car.
>
> He was wearing an Armani suit and drove a red Ferrari.

Some dull adjectives—and other words to avoid

actually
basically
empowerment
focused
holistic approach
key
logistical
nice
major
meaningful
process
scenario
upcoming
very

Do you feel holistically empowered?

From bland to vivid …

Capture the feeling with a word

Avoid bland words. When writing minutes or an article, see what a difference you can create by avoiding a nondescript word such as 'said'.

> Daphne said that the proposal was a good idea.
>
> Daphne declared that the proposal was a good idea.
>
> Daphne mentioned that the proposal was a good idea.

Use alliteration and assonance

> We excel at ideas, imagination, and innovation.
>
> We can change by evolution or by revolution.

Use repetition creatively

> ... a government of all the people, by all the people, for all the people ... (Theodore Parker, 1850)

Surprise with comparisons

> Installing new software can be like trying to stick a jelly to the ceiling.
>
> The meeting was as useful as an hour in a traffic jam.

Use word order effectively

Spoken words, in particular, have more power at the start or end of the sentence. Use that fact to your advantage.

> Down went profits again last year.
>
> Exciting ideas have been put forward by members.

Fact

Assonance

Assonance is when the vowels in nearby words have a similar sound which create a kind of echo, such as:
easy to please
rain and hail
sonnet and porridge

'All day the wind blows low with mellow tone'

Tennyson's 'The Lotus-Eaters'

Alliteration

Alliteration is when the same letter or sound occurs at the beginning of adjacent or closely connected words, such as:
cool, calm, and collected

'Whereat, with blade, with bloody blameful blade, He bravely broached his boiling bloody breast.'

A Midsummer Night's Dream (Act V, sc.i)

14 How technology can help you

See Ch. 5, First steps

Warning!
Always keep a clean copy of the text you are editing, so that you can refer back to it.

Want to know more?
Style guides; Ch. 4
First steps; Ch. 5
Style and tone; Ch. 9
Accuracy; Ch. 10
Brevity; Ch. 11
Clarity; Ch. 12

If the text you are to edit is sent to you electronically or on a disk you have the option of doing your editing on screen. If you plan to do this, it is worth investing time in discovering how your word processor can help you.

However, note the comments in the earlier section on first steps and always keep an on-system copy of the original, which you can refer back to.

Also, remember that an on-paper edit is a good way of noticing different aspects of the text which you may want to change. If a document is ultimately to be read on paper, it is best to make at least one of the edits on a paper version.

Some word-processing functions are particularly useful if you edit a document as part of a team.

Remember ...

■ When applying software checks to your text, avoid automatically following their advice.

■ Some programmes do not differentiate between what is *wrong* and what is *preferred*.

■ No matter how much you rely on your word processor, never rely on it to pick up all the mistakes.

■ Always check by eye as well as by computer.

Check the manual

- As systems vary, refer to your user manual for more information on the options available to you.

- Most word-processing packages allow you to choose whether they check your work as a separate step, or as you write the text.

- You may choose to work on text with some facilities such as the spelling checker running all the time.

- You may prefer to apply these functions as a separate activity.

- The way you work is a personal decision.

Spelling checkers

- Your system is able to spell check for different versions of English, including United Kingdom, American, Australian, and Canadian. Make sure your computer is set to the correct version for you.

- A spelling checker checks for mistakes such as incorrect spelling or words run together.

- It will *not* let you know which of alternative correct spellings you should use in context, such as 'practice' or 'practise', 'it's' or 'its'.

- Some systems have a 'sounds like' facility which will check for similar-sounding words.

- Word processors do not know if you should type 'form' instead of 'from', or 'now' instead of 'not'. They can check what you wrote, not what you intended to write.

- The checker will almost certainly spot accidentally repeated words in text. However, it will not be able to tell you if you have omitted a word.

> **Watch out!**
> Your spelling checker will tell you if you have repeated a word twice.
> That makes it difficult to advise editors: always check the text by reading it thoroughly.

■ If there are specialist words you use frequently, such as a club, author, or product name, you can add them to the dictionary.

■ Be cautious about systems which are shared with others, as it is perfectly feasible that they have added a wrong spelling to the dictionary.

Find and replace

This function allows you to replace all your misuses of a certain word in one go. So, if you discover that you have misspelt the name of a scientist or author, you can instruct it to find every reference to 'Pastuer' and change it to 'Pasteur'. Be careful, as your word could appear in other contexts, or be contained within another word. If you change 'Wild' to 'Wilde', you would also change a sentence beginning 'Wild flowers'.

Hyphenation dictionaries

Some software packages have hyphenation dictionaries which tell you where words should break. You can override these if you want to.

Grammar checkers

A grammar checker may help you spot grammatical errors, such as a singular verb with a plural subject or the misuse of 'that' and 'which'. Treat the suggestions with caution. The techniques they apply are quite simple, and as a result the advice may not always be correct in context. They will also suggest you change use of the passive voice to the active. This is good to do, but it is a *style change*, not a *grammar correction*.

Writing style

Style checkers look for points which the program considers incorrect, including the passive voice. They also calculate the readability of text by looking at the number of long words to a sentence. The program will draw attention to these points of

Watch out!
Technology is improving all the time, but grammar checkers cannot yet understand what you *meant* to say. They'll only check what you *have* said.

You wrote:
New rules have been introduced by the Club

Grammar checkers suggest:
The Club has introduced new rules

style, and may offer you an alternative. Some systems allow you to choose a style such as 'normal' or 'technical'. You can also customize a style for the document you are working on.

Readability scores

Some programmes calculate a readability score which shows how easy it is to understand the text. They are a useful guide, but can be time-consuming to apply. Most of them do a basic calculation which looks at word length and sentence length.

Many editors find it more effective to read the text slowly, so that they 'hear' it in their heads. This helps them to notice long sentences, difficult vocabulary, and clumsy constructions.

Thesaurus

If your word processor includes a thesaurus you can use it to make text more interesting if the same word keeps appearing. Be cautious about misusing words or making the text over-complex.

Most people find that a thesaurus in book or CD form is more useful than the one offered on their system. They certainly offer a wider range of suggestions.

Auto-correct

If you are editing as part of a team, see whether an automatic text function will help you to ensure consistency. This would typically cover standard paragraphs or sentences. Once agreed, they become stored as part of your template.

Templates

Templates are a way of customizing a document to help you ensure consistency. They are particularly useful if you work as part of a team. If everyone submits text to the editor in a standard format, much of the chore of the task is removed.

Quick tip
To check your readability, work out your average number of long words to a sentence. For most occupations, it shouldn't be more than three.

Where certain information must always be included, such as the title, date, and edition number of a newsletter, this can form part of your template.

Highlighting

A system highlighter is like a pen. It will highlight text which you believe you, or the original writer, should change.

Tracking changes

This is a useful function for anyone editing or working on text which was written by another person. By using the tracking mechanism you can mark the changes you are suggesting. This may be by:

■ underlining;

■ printing on screen in a different colour;

■ putting an indicator line at the side of the page.

The originator of the text then has the option of accepting or rejecting the changes. Most systems with this facility show the name of the person suggesting the change, and the date.

Comment or annotate

This aspect of the software allows editors to insert comments on text. The comments remain masked from view, so they are not distracting. When you are ready to consider the comments in more depth, you can recall them.

You can use this feature to collect comments from a number of people. Each comment will include the initials of the person who made it.

Tracking changes

This is a useful function for anyone who is editing or working on text which was written by another person. By using the tracking mechanism you can mark the changes you are suggesting. This may be by:

❏ underlining;

❏ printing on screen in a different colour;

❏ putting an indicator line at the side of the page.

The originator of the text then has the option of accepting or rejecting the changes. Most of the systems with this facility show the name of the person suggesting the change, and the date.

Comment or annotate

This aspect of the software allows editors to insert comments on text. The comments remain masked from view, so they are not distracting. When you are ready to consider the comments in more depth, you can recall them.

You can use this feature to collect comments from a number of people. Each comment will include the initials of the person who made itthe corrections.

[0] I think you have made a perfect job of editing this. Well done!

Section B
Contents

The editor's toolkit

Whether editing on screen or on paper, before you start assemble the tools you may need to do the job.

For reference

☐ original draft, brief, or essay title

☐ sources of information

☐ style guide or guides

☐ dictionary and spelling dictionary

☐ thesaurus

For making changes

☐ pens: red, blue, green

☐ highlighters

☐ pencils

☐ notepads

☐ adhesive notelets

☐ index cards

For practical tasks

☐ scissors, paste, adhesive tape

☐ stapler and spare staples

☐ eraser

☐ hole-punch

☐ ruler

For double-checking

☐ calculator

The 'editing contract'

When working on text by others, it's worth having a discussion with them before they begin as the basis for an 'editing contract'. This is a chance to clarify what all those concerned expect, so that writers understand what *may* be changed, and editors understand what they *can* change.

The 'contract' is particularly useful if the text may need to be changed a lot. By clarifying the situation before work begins, you may save time and disagreement later. The 'contract' could establish any of the following points which are relevant.

☐ Who the primary readers are: who is the text for?

☐ Other people who may receive the document.

☐ The purpose: why it is being produced.

☐ The practicalities: the word count, the deadline, and when the text will be published.

☐ State of the text: whether it is a draft or final version.

☐ Content: what must be included or omitted.

☐ Illustrations: you may want to suggest charts, tabulations, or photos. If writers think you only want words, they will only send words.

☐ The style: provide your style guide including sentence length, word choice, level of formality.

At this stage you can also discuss:

☐ Whether the writer should obtain approvals, such as from a manager, or copyright permissions.

☐ Who has the right to make changes.

☐ Who has the ultimate responsibility for the text.

☐ Whether and when they will see changes.

Know your readers: a checklist

These are some of the points about your readers which you should consider. For the particular text you are working on, there may be other points as well.

Your readers' knowledge

☐ What is their educational level?

☐ How good is their use of English?

Your answers to these questions will influence the language you use, your approach, and the level of understanding you aim for.

See Ch.3 for dealing with diverse readers and Part B for editing the technical for the non-technical

Other points about your readers' knowledge

☐ What do they *want* to know?

☐ What might they *need* to know?

☐ How much do they already know about the subject?

☐ What technical or specialist knowledge do they have? It is essential to know this if they are not to be bored or confused by the text.

Your readers' attitude

☐ How interested are they in the subject matter?

☐ Are they likely to have strong opinions or prejudices about the subject, such as disagreeing with the main argument?

☐ How do they feel about you or your organization?

☐ Have they always felt that way, or is the feeling new?

☐ If it's new, why? Have they changed, or have you?

☐ How busy are they? A busy person may prefer text presented as bullet points, rather than paragraphs.

How will your readers use the document?

☐ Do they plan to condense it into another document, such as a monthly report?

☐ Will they discuss it in a meeting?

☐ Might they use it as the basis of a presentation?

How do they prefer to receive information?

☐ Do they prefer to receive information on paper or electronically?

☐ Would they prefer a long and continuous piece of text, or a number of short pieces?

☐ Would they prefer detailed statistics, such as a tabulation, or would a graph or pie chart serve the purpose better?

Other questions you may need to answer

☐ What age are the readers? This is particularly important if, for example, the text is about pensions or other age-related subjects.

☐ What gender are the readers? This is particularly important for addresses and salutations in letters.

Style guides

A style guide is a document which lists the answers to a mass of questions which editors and writer-editors often ask themselves while they are working. It may form part of a larger, formal document produced by a company, a corporate rule book which must be followed, or a few sheets of paper which help individuals to edit.

The advantages of a style guide are:

☐ It saves time because there are fewer decisions to make while editing.

☐ You can obtain approval for its suggestions, which cuts down on arguments.

☐ When several people work together, for example a group who all send out correspondence, it helps the organization to appear consistent and efficient.

Creating your own style guide

See Ch. 3, Readers and aims

Whether you work on your own on newsletters or essays, or as part of a group, it is worth investing time in creating a style guide.

See Ch. 4, Style guides

If you work in an area such as company communications, you may need to create slightly varying style guides for different publications.

See following page for style guide checklist

Every editor will have his or her own requirements from a style guide, but the following pages give an idea of some of the areas you may need to consider,

Many newspapers and periodicals publish books which set out the style guidelines they follow. This is a useful starting point for creating your own style guide. Alternatively, you could produce a guide of your own and, if appropriate, get it approved. It will save everyone time.

Style guide checklist

See Ch. 14, How technology can help you

☐ Abbreviations: *USA* or *U.S.A*?

☐ *And* or *&*: where there's a choice, which do you use?

☐ Bullet point lists: are you using capitals at the start, or semi-colons at the end?

☐ Capitals: which words receive capitals? *Sales Manager* or *sales manager*?

☐ Contractions: can you use *it's*, or must you use *it is*?

☐ Currencies: do you write: *$3* or *$3.00*; *$0.50* or *50c*?

☐ Dates: do you write *4 April* or *4ᵗʰ April* or *April 4ᵗʰ*?

☐ email: how do you express this? *email*, or *e-mail*? And procedural decisions about salutations and sign-offs.

☐ Emphasis: do you emphasise a word with: **bold**, *italics*, or <u>underlining</u>?

☐ Figures or words – *ten* or *10*? *two hundred* or *200*?

☐ Grammatical points: can you use *and* or *but*, etc. at start of sentence? Can you split infinitives?

☐ Hyphens: do you break words at line ends? Which words do you hyphenate? Which do you treat as one word?

☐ Italics for foreign words? *in situ* or in situ?

☐ Jargon: a list of words you can and cannot use; definitions of terminology.

☐ Names: do you use the title (*Mr/Mrs*) or not? full names or initials? In articles or essays, full name (*Jane Austen*) or family name only (*Austen*)?

☐ Numbering: how do you number sections of reports, minutes, and other documents?

☐ Percentages: do you use per cent; or %; how do you express a range of percentages (8–9% or *8% – 9%*)?

☐ Preferred vocabulary: do you prefer *while* or *whilst*? *among* or *amongst*?

☐ Proper nouns: treatment of club and company names, including possessives and abbreviations.

☐ References and bibliographies: how do you style them?

☐ Honours, qualifications, and titles: do you use them? How do you express them? *OBE* or *O.B.E.*? *M.D.* or *MD*?

☐ Quotation and speech marks: do you use single '*Help!*' or double "*Ouch!*" in your text?

☐ Sentences and paragraphs: what is the preferred length for specific documents and readers?

☐ Spellings: particular difficulties and preferred option when there's a choice (*dispatch/despatch, benefited/benefitted*).

☐ Symbols: particularly in scientific writing, such as temperatures.

☐ Telephone numbers: how do you express them?

☐ Times: do you write *10.30 am* or *a.m.*; *3.30* or *1530*?

☐ Weights and measures: how do you express them? yards or metres? miles or kilometres?

Visual aspects

Decide the style you wish to follow for:

☐ typefaces in body text

☐ headings, headline, sub-headings

☐ layout

☐ captions, figure headings

Standard letters

Word processors have made standard letters a part of many people's working lives as they are so quick and easy. However, there can be disadvantages. It's tempting to take less trouble with standard letters than with individual letters.

If you are doing a 'mail merge', which sends the same letter to many people with each one personalized, make sure the process has been carefully checked before you start. If the correlation between the letter and the database in not perfect, your letter could begin: 'Dear Mr 6 Station Road'.

Points to check if you work with standard letters

☐ Is all the content relevant to the situation?

☐ Is the tone correct, as well as the content?

☐ Has everything that should be altered been altered, including the date and the name of the recipient?

☐ Is there any repetition or inconsistency, especially if the letter was created by choosing sections from a list of standard paragraphs?

☐ Does the letter look tidy, particularly if it has been completed by hand (such as in ticking boxes)?

Remember the relationship

Standard letters do not help to build relationships, particularly if they include alternatives, such as 'Sir/Madam' or 'house/flat', or general phrases such as 'your recent communication'.

Once every year or so

Standard letters become old-fashioned if they are not updated regularly, and sometimes people ignore a communication when they see it's the same old letter. So, about once a year or so, set aside some time to freshen up the standard letters.

Checklist for letters and faxes

As well as checking your letter and faxes for:

☐ contents

☐ style

☐ accuracy

☐ brevity

☐ clarity

you will need to check some additional points.

Can you answer 'yes' to all these questions?

☐ Have you included your reference, and theirs?

☐ Is the date correct?

☐ If answering a letter, have you used their reference?

☐ Have you used a suitable and helpful heading?

☐ If the letter is confidential, have you made that clear?

☐ Have you used people's titles and qualifications correctly?

☐ Have your correctly paired Dear Sir/Dear Madam with Yours faithfully; Dear Maria/Dear Mr Jones with Yours sincerely?

☐ Have you ended with your full name, and title?

... and on faxes:

☐ Is the level of formality correct for the message?

☐ Are you absolutely certain you are sending it to the right number?

☐ Have you used a confidentiality warning, in case it goes to the wrong person?

Checklist for emails

So far there's no 'etiquette' for emails, and organizations have their own practices for starting and ending messages: some use salutations and endings, and some do not.

Overall, two types of email seem to have developed:

- ☐ the informal message, which is an electronic equivalent to a note put on a colleague's desk

- ☐ the formal communication, which is as full and precise as a paper version of the same information.

The speed and apparent informality of emails make it particularly important to check the details.

You should be able to answer 'yes' to all these questions

- ☐ If responding to a message, have you checked that you have not accidentally done a 'reply to all'?

- ☐ Is your email polite and respectful to the recipient and any anyone else it mentions?

- ☐ Would you be happy if your email were seen by your boss? It may be.

- ☐ If you've abbreviated words, will the reader still understand your message easily?

- ☐ If you have omitted punctuation, will the reader still understand your message easily?

- ☐ Does it reflect you as a person and show that you are capable of high-quality work?

- ☐ If you are sending formatted text, are you sure your software is compatible with the recipient's?

- ☐ With formal messages, have you also applied the Letters checklist?

Editing minutes

See *One Step Ahead: Organizing and Participating in Meetings*, in this series

There are many differences between editing minutes and editing other forms of communication. Editors of minutes should make sure that they follow the traditions of their organization.

How minutes are different

☐ they must contain certain information

☐ they tend to be more formal

☐ they tend to use the passive voice

Check that essential information is included

☐ name of organization

☐ name of committee, if relevant

☐ date and time of meeting

☐ venue of meeting

☐ list of attendees, including the chair and the secretary

Check that all the essential sections are included

☐ apologies for absence

☐ minutes of last meeting

☐ matters arising

☐ business discussion

☐ any other business

☐ date of next meeting

Check the content

The amount of detail needed varies from committee to committee.

- ☐ At formal meetings, such as annual general meetings, the minutes are often just a record of decisions made and actions to be taken.

- ☐ Some minutes are almost word-for-word accounts of proceedings.

- ☐ Most minutes fall somewhere in between these extremes.

Whatever style of minutes you edit

- ☐ Always include a record of decisions, with the names of the proposer and seconder at formal meetings.

- ☐ Always record who agrees to do what, and by what date.

Check the style

For most types of writing there is a trend toward less formal communication, but minutes may be more formal. Check that the style is appropriate.

- ☐ Formal: 'A comment was made that … ' or 'It was thought …'.

- ☐ Informal: 'David commented that …' or 'The members thought …'.

Check the numbering

- ☐ Check the numbering of points and pages. The numbering should follow the sequence of the agenda.

Technical style

☐ Be meticulous about following the guidelines for clear communications

☐ Never use jargon.

☐ Use adjectives: colour, shape, size.

☐ Use descriptive phrases.

☐ Be explicit, even if you are confident that users will get your meaning.

☐ Comment on the fact, for example, that a number is higher or lower than expected.

☐ Show connections between facts: 'even', 'although', 'however'.

☐ Differentiate between new information and familiar information.

☐ Use judicious repetition – summaries, recaps, grand summaries.

☐ Repeat nouns if you need to: in technical editing, clarity is more important than style.

On the page

☐ Use headings and sub-headings to break down the information.

☐ Give informative titles to all diagrams.

☐ Put as much information on diagrams as is needed – no more.

☐ Use a simple numbering system.

☐ Use 'run-on' sentences at page turns so that users do not miss parts of explanations.

☐ Avoid long paragraphs.

Editing the technical for the non-technical

The principles

- [ ] Always involve a user in the process.

- [ ] Think how the user will work with the text: at a desk, or under a car?

- [ ] Ensure every step is explained.

- [ ] Describe what the user can see, whether it's on the screen or in the engine.

Technical content

- [ ] Include all the essential steps.

- [ ] Explain unfamiliar ideas.

- [ ] Explain the significance of facts and figures.

- [ ] Make connections with what's already familiar.

- [ ] Exclude anything that is not relevant.

- [ ] Do not elaborate on the obvious.

- [ ] Do not emphasize points of secondary importance.

Technical order

- [ ] Use a logical order: create a 'map' for the 'traveller'.

- [ ] Consider what will help: purpose, then mechanical details, or the other way round.

- [ ] Provide the right information at the right time.

- [ ] Be cautious when using glossaries, brackets, and footnotes.

- [ ] Do not rely on overuse of cross-referencing.

- [ ] Use contents pages and indexes.

See Chs. 11 and 12 on Brevity and Clarity

Editing the text of newsletters

☐ Try to make sure that every edition of your newsletter has something in it for all the different sorts of people who read it.

☐ Make sure news stories carry the main facts in the first paragraphs. That is, make sure you answer the questions Who? What? When? Where? Why? How?

☐ Put the detail toward the end, so that if people stop reading, they will still have the main facts.

☐ Give your longer, background stories an attention-grabbing opening and an equally strong end. Good openings – and endings – include quotations, anecdotes, surprising facts, and challenging statements.

☐ Keep the stories short. Look for ways to divide a long story into two. And see whether detailed information can be treated as a separate piece on the same page.

☐ Remember that quotations from people can really bring a publication to life. Always say who the speaker is, and why their comments on the subject are relevant.

☐ Use good headlines. Traditionally, headlines are short, with an active verb. But they may also be a chance to apply some humour, alliteration, or plays on words.

☐ Make sure all your photos have interesting captions that are more than just a label. A well-captioned photo can persuade people to read the article which accompanies it.

See Copyright and Plagiarism information on p. 127

☐ Remember, the law applies just as much to an informal, local newsletter or an internal publication as it does to a newspaper.

Editing a document as a team

Before writing starts

- ☐ Clarify readership and aims.
- ☐ Appoint an overall editor.
- ☐ Know who is responsible for what.
- ☐ Make deadlines clear.
- ☐ Arrange progress meetings.
- ☐ Create and distribute a style guide.
- ☐ Decide work methods.
- ☐ Ensure all technologies are compatible.

Editing on screen

See Ch. 12, Clarity

- ☐ Keep a clean copy.
- ☐ Use cut-and-paste facility.
- ☐ Highlight changes so that everyone can see them.
- ☐ Make use of change-tracking tools.

Editing on paper

- ☐ Keep a clean copy or several copies.
- ☐ Make sure you have your 'editor's toolkit'.
- ☐ Keep changes tidy so that others can see them.
- ☐ Mark changes in the text and in the margin.

Working with figures

Presenting figures is an important part of the work of editors and writer-editors. The task is hard because some practices are so common that they are almost rules; in other areas you have to decide what to do, such as whether to use 'per cent' or '%'.

Principles

☐ Make sure the numbers are meaningful: people often want stories or trends, not numbers.

☐ Be careful about over precision: A4 paper is 210 x 297 mm. For most purposes 210 x 300 mm is fine.

☐ If appropriate, round off figures and explain that is what you have done.

☐ When dealing with currencies, use common denominations where possible.

☐ Show the currency or measurement quoted.

☐ If currency has been converted, give the rate applied.

☐ Where appropriate, quote sources, with the year.

☐ Do not start a sentence with a figure: write it out or rewrite the sentence: not '1999 ...' , but 'In 1999 ...'.

See also
Ch. 2 on different circumstances, Ch. 4 on style guides,

Checking tables

Give as much attention to tables as to the rest of the document, bearing the following in mind:

☐ It's easier to compare numbers vertically than horizontally.

☐ Do not over 'over-box' your figures.

☐ Ensure decimals line up.

☐ Make sure every column is adequately headed.

☐ Put units in the heading, not in the column.

Numbers advice

See Ch. 16, How technology can help you

Working with figures

This checklist is based on advice given to financial journalists.

☐ Spell out numbers one to nine; then use *10, 11, 12*, etc.

☐ Follow the same rule for ordinals: *second*, 14th.

However, use figures if your are dealing with:

☐ measurements: *1 mile, 7 per cent, 9 a.m.*

☐ ranges of numbers: *9–12 months.*

☐ fractions, decimals: *$2^1/_2$, 2.5 months*

Expressing fractions and ranges of numbers

☐ Write out fractions: *two-thirds, one-tenth.*

☐ Most people prefer *per cent* to *%*.

☐ Write *£5m–£10m* (not *£5–10m*).

☐ Write *10,000–12,000* (not *10–12,000*).

☐ Write *3m–4m* (not *3–4m*).

☐ Express ratios as *nine to seven, 17 to 24*, or *17:24*.

☐ Express periods as *1949 to 1963* or *during 1949–63.*

Dealing with large numbers

See Ch. 4 on style guides and checklists in Part B

Newspaper research shows people prefer:

☐ millions expressed as *10m, 7.2m*

☐ abbreviations: *1.5 million*, not *1,500,000*

☐ *500,000*, rather than *half a million*

And larger still? In the UK and US:

☐ A billion is 1,000 million; write *2bn, 3.9bn*

☐ A trillion is a million million, but *2,000bn* is clearer than *2 trillion.*

Contents checklist

You should be able to answer 'yes' to all these questions:

☐ Are all the facts right?

☐ Have you double-checked names, dates, and numbers?

☐ Have you provided all the necessary examples or supporting details?

☐ Are all the loose ends tied up?

☐ Are all the statements accurate and logical?

☐ Is uncertainty shown by such words as *perhaps*, *probably*, *some authorities believe*?

☐ Are all ideas covered thoroughly?

☐ Is all the information technically correct?

☐ Have you differentiated between fact and opinion?

☐ Are you confident that all your readers will understand the content?

☐ Have you expressed ideas visually where possible?

☐ Have you divided the text into sections to aid understanding?

You should be able to answer 'no' to all these questions:

☐ Does the text give the impression that it is trying to impress the reader, rather than express opinions or present a case?

☐ Does the text include anything that is not relevant?

☐ Have you assumed readers have knowledge which they may not have?

Style checklist

You should be able to answer 'yes' to all these questions:

See Ch. 4 on style guides and checklists in Part B

☐ Does the text read well?

☐ Is the style appropriate for the purpose?

☐ Does the text have the right degree of formality or informality?

☐ Does the text begin in a way that makes the reader want to read on?

☐ Are the sentences constructed in a clear and straightforward way?

☐ Is the vocabulary varied and interesting?

☐ Have you always used the simplest words for the job?

☐ Are ideas or words repeated effectively?

☐ Are the paragraphs of an appropriate length?

☐ Have you kept the text lively by varying the sentence length?

☐ Have you cut every redundant word from the text?

☐ Do you sound objective and sincere?

☐ Have you used links and transitions to help the text flow?

You should be able to answer 'no' to all these questions:

☐ Do you have any long, rambling sentences that may confuse the reader?

☐ Is there any careless or monotonous repetition?

☐ Will some of the readers consider that the text contains jargon?

Accuracy checklist

When checking for accuracy, always:

☐ Check spellings with a spell checker if you are working electronically, and with a spelling dictionary if you are working on paper.

☐ Check for confusable words such as (principle and principal; advice and advise).

☐ Check any spellings special to your piece of text such as scientific terminology.

In addition, pay special attention to:

☐ names of people, places, organizations;

☐ statistics, dates, numbering;

☐ consistency.

Also make sure that you:

☐ check for grammar mistakes;

☐ use your grammar checker if you find it helps;

☐ check the punctuation.

Become familiar with your most frequent mistakes and check for those errors separately. Many people miss the following:

☐ ambiguous statements;

☐ inconsistencies, such as the use of abbreviations;

☐ errors in headings and headlines;

☐ errors in references and captions;

☐ wrong use of typefaces;

☐ grammatical errors;

☐ typographical errors;

☐ punctuation errors.

Brevity checklist

Can you answer 'yes' to all these questions?

☐ Are all the facts necessary?

☐ Is everything appropriate for the intended readership?

☐ Is everything appropriate for the document's purpose?

☐ Does every paragraph really have to be included?

☐ Is every sentence playing an important role in the paragraph?

☐ Is every word really needed in each sentence?

Can you answer 'no' to all these questions?

☐ Does the text contain long phrases where short ones would work better?

☐ Are there any long words which could be replaced by short ones?

☐ Has the text become so brief that there could be misunderstanding or confusion?

☐ Have you omitted essential explanations or definitions?

☐ Is the text too densely crammed with facts?

Are there any instances of the following?

☐ sections where the text rambles;

☐ wasted words;

☐ compound verbs;

☐ phrases that could be replaced with a single word;

☐ instances of inelegant or lazy repetition.

See Ch. 14, How technology can help you

See Part B, Know your Weaknesses, for a list of frequent accuracy oversights

Clarity checklist

Can you answer 'yes' to all these questions?

The sentences

☐ Are the sentences clear?

☐ Is the average sentence length between 15 and 20 words?

☐ If not, is the text for readers who will be happy with longer sentences?

The sentence structure

☐ Does the sentence structure add to the clarity?

☐ Does it contain active verbs whenever appropriate?

☐ Have you expressed the meaning in a positive way, rather than a negative way?

☐ If not, does the text aim to emphasize the negative?

The word choice

☐ Does the text contain the most appropriate words throughout?

☐ Is the text made up of everyday words, rather than more complex words?

☐ If not, is there every reason to believe that the words the text contains are best for the readers?

☐ Does the text contain lots of verbs?

And finally

☐ Can you honestly say that the text aims to express the writer's thoughts, rather than impress the reader by using language in a fussy and complex way?

Word and phrases to help you 'flow'

Signposting the route

☐ To start with … I will then …

☐ There are three issues/points/problems …

☐ In this section …

☐ I will describe the … in three stages. Firstly, …

See Ch. 11, Brevity

Moving on

☐ Following this …

☐ Then …

☐ The next step …

☐ This also suggests …

☐ For example/For instance …

☐ Another possibility/factor/example …

☐ Thus …

☐ And so …

Reinforcing

☐ Furthermore, …

☐ As I pointed out in …

☐ Looking again at …

☐ Again, …

☐ Also, …

☐ In addition …

☐ Nevertheless, …

☐ Alongside these …

☐ It should be borne in mind that …

See Ch. 12, Clarity

Word and phrases to help you 'flow'

See Ch. 3, Readers and aims

Changing direction

☐ On the other hand, …

☐ Meanwhile, …

☐ However, …

☐ In contrast, …

☐ We/I will now turn to …

☐ In comparison …

☐ Despite this …

☐ Another possibility/interpretation …

Introducing questions or doubt

☐ Alternatively, …

☐ However, …

☐ Although …

☐ But …

☐ In spite of this, …

☐ Even so, …

☐ Yet, …

Concluding

☐ Two questions remain.

☐ The question remains, does …?

☐ In concluding …

☐ Finally, …

☐ One final point …

☐ If we now summarize the …

☐ In conclusion, …

Copyright

The only people who have the right to copy a piece of text is the person who wrote it and those to whom they have given permission. This is their copyright, and it is protected by laws. These vary from country to country, but there are international conventions.

You can *normally* copy *small* amounts of text for personal study. You *can* copy the work of authors who died some time ago (in Europe, 70 years). Many institutions buy a licence allowing those working there to make more extensive copies.

So before you copy anything written by someone else, make sure that you are legally entitled to do so. This covers any kind of copying – even writing an extract out by hand.

Before you copy anything written by someone else, make sure that you are legally entitled to do so.

Plagiarism

Plagiarism is using others' intellectual work and passing it off as your own. It is an extremely serious academic offence. If you use sentences, phrases, or expressions from any source, you *must* acknowledge your source. In certain cases, thoughts which you have paraphrased will also be plagiarism.

Always quote the name of the person and publication quoted *and* put the quoted words or phrases in quotation marks.

With sources, you must be specific. It is not enough to mention the publication in your bibliography.

Plagiarism is an extremely serious academic offence.

Defamation

Defamation includes libel, which is writing something about a person which is not true. There's a fine line between a libel and expressing an opinion. Deciding whether something is libel makes lawyers rich. Use your judgement. If it is not true, supportable, and capable of being proved, do not write or say it.

If it is not true, supportable and capable of being proved, do not write or say it.

Proof checking: prepare and manage the task

Get prepared

☐ Proofread in a conducive environment.

☐ Work for short stretches—build in breaks.

☐ If possible, avoid proofing when you're tired.

☐ Have a dictionary and style guide to hand.

☐ Enlarge small copy before proofreading it.

☐ Proofread on double-spaced hard copy.

☐ Make a back-up copy before starting.

☐ Copy the text onto tinted paper to keep your senses awake.

Manage the process

☐ Survey the entire document before starting.

☐ Break the task into sections.

☐ Read the text aloud to involve an extra sense.

☐ When comparing copy, read to a partner or a tape.

☐ Read each word letter by letter.

☐ Use magnifying rulers, index cards with windows.

☐ Read backwards if you are particularly concerned about spotting typos and spelling errors.

☐ Highlight errors before using proofreading symbols.

☐ Use standard proofreading symbols.

☐ Make proofreading a game with challenges and rewards.

☐ Know your own weak spots.

Proofs: know your weaknesses

These are some of the most common mistakes which people overlook when they are proof-checking:

☐ errors in headings and headlines

☐ transpositions of words or letters

☐ letters omitted from words

☐ words omitted from sentences

☐ letters repeated in words

☐ repeated words, particularly at line ends

☐ words wrongly hyphenated

☐ errors in facts, figures, dates, etc.

☐ oddities in proper nouns overlooked

☐ inconsistencies

☐ grammatically incorrect sentences

☐ spelling mistakes

☐ wrongly punctuated sentences

☐ wrong spacing after punctuation marks

☐ capitals used wrongly or inconsistently

☐ undefined abbreviations and acronyms

☐ errors in photo captions or diagram numbering

☐ confusion with words with more than one spelling

☐ capitals used wrongly or inconsistently

☐ undefined abbreviations and acronyms

☐ inconsistencies in punctuation, particularly in lists

☐ extra spaces between words

☐ wrong use of typefaces

See following pages for the most frequently used symbols, and those symbols in use

Proof-checking symbols

There are dozens of proof-checking symbols. These are some of the most useful. When you are proof checking, always:

☐ Keep a clean copy, in case your changes get messy.

☐ Use a red pen, or another clearly visible colour.

☐ Show the alteration in both the text and the margin.

Use this symbol in the margin

insert⟨

deleted

leave unchanged

change CAPS to lower case

change lower case to caps

indent

remove indent

run on close up

paragraph break

start a new paragraph. Alternatively,

change to bold

change to italics

change to roman type

words or transpose characters

Proof-checking symbols in use

Editing *often* means different things to different people. The editor of a newspaper or magazine will be responsible for content, appearance, and the view it takes on certain issues. These editors ~~will~~ decide which groups of people they want to read the publication, HOW they will attract them. They will consider the style of writing to be used, how complex the ~~information~~ should be and the extent to which they will use photographs, illustrations and cartoons.

For other people, editing means going through something they have written to make sure that it's as good as they can possibly make it.

they could be dealing with letters, essays, reports, or electronic media including emails and websites. Between these two extremes are all the other people involved in editing in-house magazines, marketing brochures, theses, newsletters, and minutes of meetings.

Good luck with your editing and revising.

⟨

⁊

⟨ *and* ≠

✓ stet

⌃⟨

⌃⟨

⌐

⌐

≡

⌐

⎍

Further reading and resources

Organizations

Popular Communication Courses Ltd, 60 High Street, Bridgenorth, Shropshire,WV16 4DX, www.popcomm.co.uk
Courses in all aspects of writing and designing text, for paper or on-screen publication.

The Plain Language Commission, The Castle, 29 Stoneheads, Whaley Bridge, High Peak, SK23 7BB
Courses and editing services with the focus on clear language.

The International Association of Business Communicators, One Hallidie Plaza, Suite 600, San Francisco, California 94102 USA www.iabc.com
Provide an internationally recognized qualification for people working in PR and Internal Communication.

The British Association of Communicators in Business, 42 Borough High Street, London, SE1 1XW www.bacb.org
Networking, courses and annual conference for those working on internal communications.

Publications

Books on language

The Oxford Dictionary for Writers and Editors, ed. R. M. Ritter (OUP, 2000) A dictionary of spellings and definitions.

Everyday Grammar, John Seely (OUP, 2001)
Explains the structure of English in a straightforward way for those who have little or no knowledge of the subject. Includes an alphabetical reference grammar.

Troublesome Words, Bill Bryson (Penguin 1997)
Deals with language, giving both English and American usage.

The Financial Times Style Guide, Paul Birch (Prentice-Hall, 1994)
Covers language and includes short sections on law, industry-specific terms, currencies, and other facts for journalists.

Writing Works, Krystyna Weinstein (Institute of Personnel and Development, 1995)
An A–Z with grammar, structures and tips for writers.

Fowler's Modern English Usage, 3rd edn, ed. R. W. Burchfield (OUP, 1996)
A detailed book for lovers of language.

Specialist books

The Newsletter Editor's Handbook, Marvin Arth, Helen Ashmore, and Elaine Floyd (Writer's Digest Books, 1997)
Deals with interviews, using quotes, contributions, and layout.

Editing Technical Writing, Donald Samson Jr (OUP, 1993)
A big and rare book for specialists, with suggestions on how to express technical information visually.

Writing at University, Phyllis Creme and Mary R. Lea (Open University, 1997)
Provides help for students at all levels on aspects of writing.

The Professional Secretary, John Spencer and Adrian Pruss (Continuum International Publishing, 2000)
Deals with agendas, minutes, and writing, as well as many other secretarial skills. Lots to read in a solid and thorough book.

Handbook for Proof-Reading, Laura Killen Anderson (NTC Business Books, 1992)
Techniques for identifying errors and use of symbols.

The Oxford Guide to Style (OUP, 2002)
All the answers you need for perfect proof checking.

The Writer's Rights, Michael Legat (A. & C. Black, 1995)
Explains copyright, plagiarism, contracts, permissions.

Chicago Manual of Style, University of Chicago Press (John Wiley, 1993)
Detailed reference book covering the American way of writing.

The Copyright, Designs and Patents Act (HMSO, 1998)

Websites

www.powa.org
Detailed site covering organizing, revising, editing, as well as the editing process. Includes help with essays.

www.englishgrammar101.com
Takes you back to the basics on grammar. Particularly keen on verb usage. Includes free grammar tutorials.

www.ucl.ac.uk/internet-grammar
Advanced site, designed for university students but useful for all. With self-check exercises.

www.electriceditors.net
Guidance on style and grammar.

www.theslot.com
Deals with the role of the editor, as well as writing, editing, and being sharp.

www.vocabula.com
On-line version of *Vocabula Review*, providing feature articles about writing.

www.bsi-global.com
This site will provide the official British Standards Institution proof checking symbols (BS5261) for a charge.

www.ideography.co.uk/proof/marks
This site provides free downloadable proof-checking symbols, based on the BSI standard but shorter and more straightforward.

www.askoxford.com
Free advice on language from the experts at Oxford University Press, including downloadable material from this book and other books in the One Step Ahead series.

Index

Note: Major sections are indicated by **bold** page numbers.